TELLING TALES

Telling Tales

Kay Murray

authorHOUSE®

AuthorHouse™
1663 Liberty Drive
Bloomington, IN 47403
www.authorhouse.com
Phone: 1-800-839-8640

First published by AuthorHouse 11/07/2011

ISBN: 978-1-4670-0082-6 (sc)
ISBN: 978-1-4670-0083-3 (ebk)

Printed in the United States of America

This book is printed on acid-free paper.

FOREWORD

There were many reasons why I decided to write this book, most of all; it was because I was excited by the challenge. I also found that I had the time to do it. I remembered how wonderful my life had been when I lived in Rhodesia. I lived there from the age of ten until I was fifteen, but the memories I have are as strong in my mind today as they were back then, more than thirty years ago. I had so many life changing experiences in those four or five years that now, when I speak to others about it, they are either in awe of what I say, or simply do not believe me. On more than one occasion, I have been told that I ought to write a book about my experiences, and so here I am doing, just that.

It has been a cathartic and cleansing process, I have cried as much as I have laughed in recording my memories. I did not realise that I still had demons to put to rest and writing this book has helped me to do that.

I was living a different life, in a wonderful environment and differing cultures, indeed, it often seemed like I was in an entirely new world! The hardships I faced were of some benefit to me, as they have shaped me into the person I have become. The people who knew me back then, may look back and see things from a different perspective. Not all of my memories are happy ones and some people may feel that I am telling tales on them. Well, to be honest, I am. A lot of time has passed, but the hurt of some events still lingers. You will see what I mean when you read my story.

If there is one thing that I want anyone to gain from reading this book, is the knowledge that no matter what happens to you in life, somehow we find the coping mechanisms needed to allow us to get through and move on. So here I am, telling tales to you, about my fun, enjoyable and sometimes dangerous years in Africa. I hope you enjoy it, like I said; there are both tears and laughter to be found in the following pages.

CONTENTS

A NEW BEGINNING

I could feel the rush of air, the heat of a very hot sun burning on the side of my face as I approached the aeroplane door. Looking outside the sunlight blinded me as it was so bright, nothing like the weak sun I had left back in Scotland, just the day before. As I stepped out onto the hot, metal airplane stairs, I could feel the warm, African breeze on my skin. There was an unfamiliar, hot, dry and dusty smell in the air. Here we were at last; this was Bulawayo, Rhodesia, my new home.

I was startled when I saw there were crowds of people at the bottom of the aeroplane steps. There were so many people! They had cameras and were waiting around the bottom of the steps capturing our arrival as we left the aeroplane. I looked out across the airport grounds and I saw the heat rising from the runway, like hot, shimmering pools of water. I walked slowly down the steps and onto the hot tarmac, along with my family and the rest of the passengers. Very soon, we were huddled into groups to have our photographs taken. Why, I wondered? I was a confused and bemused ten-year-old. What was going on? People soon surrounded me, there were so many questions, how was the landing, did we enjoy the flight? I had no idea that at that moment in time I was part of history in the making.

Our flight from London was on a Boeing 747 Jumbo Jet aeroplane that had just landed for the first time at Bulawayo airport. Although the aeroplane had been flying for about two years, it had not yet landed at this airport, until today. The city was immensely proud of that fact and wanted to share the moment with as many people as possible. That was why there were so many reporters and photographers, asking people questions and taking photographs, all of them trying to get the most information to write the best articles for their newspapers.

The following morning we were front-page news, and right in the middle of the main photo, was me! Although it was another couple of weeks before I saw the picture for myself, when a friend at my new school showed me the picture.

Very soon, we were crowded into a large, stuffy building. This was the airport terminus and it was not much more than a vast open planned hall with checking-in/out desks and large windows down the side of the building, facing the stationery planes on the runway. The building was poorly vented and there was no air-conditioning either, there were several large fans dotted about, although they seemed to have little effect in cooling the stifling heat indoors. Someone from my father's new workplace was there to welcome us. He very quickly guided us through the terminal and then whisked us off to The Carlton Hotel, Bulawayo.

The drive to the city was much quicker than I expected and soon we arrived at our hotel. We stayed there for two weeks while my parents looked for a house to rent and bought a car. As my father had an engineering job to come to, we just needed to find a new home and settle in. The hotel was pleasant enough, a bit loud and rowdy at night, particularly at weekends, but it was otherwise a nice place to stay.

It seemed to my young, naïve eyes that it was a rather grandiose place, but then I had never really spent any time in a hotel before. There was plenty of hotel staff to help us, there were porters to help with luggage, waiters for taking orders for drinks and/or food as well as serving them when they arrived. Most of the staff were black or coloured people, apart from the managers and a couple of ladies I had seen in the reception area. I remember the carpeting being luxurious, the richest colours I had ever seen in a carpet and so thick that it felt as though I was walking on cushions. My only other memories of carpeting were of the well-used, worn and thin carpets that we had in our previous homes.

On the first night, I went off exploring and found the TV Room; there were a handful of guests seated quietly watching a large television, which was on one side of the room. They quickly ushered me into the room and with a sea of smiling faces I found I had another warm welcome. I asked if I could join them but before I could answer one of the ladies had pointed out a chair out for me to sit on. I sat down in a large, deep armchair to watch the latest episode of The Saint, which was very popular at the time. I felt quite grown up, watching TV and chatting with the older guests.

Our first evening meal is one I will always remember. When we arrived at the hotel restaurant we were greeted by waiters in smart black and white uniforms. The room was large and there were several tables with guests already eating their meals. We were shown to our table in the middle of the room by one of the waiters, in his smart uniform and crisp white shirt. He pulled a chair out for each of us, pushing the seat back under the table as we took our chairs. When I looked at the table with its brilliant white table-cloth, I saw that there was an awful lot of cutlery at each place setting. I had never seen so many knives and forks, and all for one person to use! My mother explained that this was something called 'silver service' and that each item of cutlery had a purpose and she would tell us what to use when our food came. It was all very confusing, but I felt very posh at the same time.

The hotel food was amazing; I was introduced to many new tastes and culinary pleasures! I have never yet tasted pumpkin as good as it tasted there! Every evening when we went down for dinner, the waiters all knew that I would want the luxurious, creamy textured, bright orange vegetable. Sadly, although it is now still one of my favourite vegetables, the flavour today just does not seem to live up to that of those early days. Another treat was being able to have a pudding after dinner each night.

I can recall the first night that my parents asked for some coffee after the meal. They were brought a coffee pot and some cups and saucers. The cups were the size of one of my tea sets; I had never seen cups so small. My mother was not very happy about it, she said that this was for some really strong coffee and that was why it was served in such small cups. I think she had expected a regular coffee in a regular sized cup.

We spent our days exploring the city and all it had to offer; we also looked at car lots to see what options there was for father to buy a new car for us. My parents would go and look at houses and come back to tell us what they had seen, it would not be long before they would decide on where we would be living. I remember the evenings in town were quiet; perhaps because I was young and went to bed early, but sometimes we would go for an evening stroll to see what the city nightlife was like. The hotel itself was usually busy; it had a disco area downstairs which played very loud music each evening.

It was on one of those early evening walks that I had my first taste of toasted cheese sandwiches, from the local Wimpy; the inside of my cheeks tingled as my taste buds were overwhelmed with yet another new taste to savour. I only ever had this treat a couple of times in the whole time I was living there, apparently the Wimpy was one of the expensive places to go for treats.

We were a family of five, when we arrived in Bulawayo, in early 1972. There was my mother, father, younger sister Lucy and younger brother Richard. Lucy was eight, two years younger than I was, Richard was just seven. I was a bossy, tomboy of a big sister, I did not intend to be so bossy, but I guess I felt that as the oldest child I had certain rights and privileges. I suspect that many oldest children grew up feeling the same way as I did. I was also the one to bear the brunt of any scolding that came our way when things went wrong, or if we were naughty. I think it was a case of 'you are the oldest and you should have known better than that to . . . .' I soon got used to that and each time I was given a telling off, I was able to switch off and ignore the cutting remarks, 'like water off a ducks back', is how many people would describe it.

At the time, Richard was the baby of the family and everyone looked out for him. He was special; well, that is what mother always said. He had been born with a heart murmur and he had epilepsy, so he was treated with kid gloves. He was well and truly mollycoddled, wrapped in cotton wool and pampered to death by my mother. Lucy and I often felt left out of her affections. Lucy was stuck in the middle, poor child, not mother's favourite, yet not the oldest like me, who was often given some responsibility in caring for the other children. I also had the privilege of going to the shop alone with my mother's shopping lists of things to buy.

Before coming over here, we had been living in Scotland and although it is a beautifully landscaped country, it was not somewhere that held pleasant memories for me. Perhaps this was because when I was five years old, my baby brother Adam had died there. He was only seven months old and had been born with severe heart problems. I adored him and would play with him all the time. He was a lovely cuddly baby, not chubby like some babies I had seen, but he was gorgeous all the same. I would tickle him and give him cuddles when he responded by laughing.

Each morning before I went to school, I would go into his room and give him a kiss before I left the house. On one particular morning I noticed he was very still, his lips were blue and there was a small amount of sick on the sheet, near his mouth. It was not unusual for him to be sick in the night so I told my mother about this and then left for school.

At school, just before we were to break for lunch, my teacher told me that I was to go straight home instead. I knew that this was bad news, and I ran most of the way home. I ran into the house, where I found my mother sitting on the edge of the couch. I saw that she looked really sad and was twisting a wad of tissues in her hand. I put my arm around her shoulder and gave her a hug.

As I sat down beside her, I said 'He's dead, isn't he?' I knew he was gone, even though I was only five years old at the time, I knew he had been getting worse and worse. It had been only a matter of time before we would have lost him.

My mother responded by floods of tears, she was unable to speak. We sat there on the couch for a long time, crying until we had no more tears left. I continued to cry, continuously, for two weeks, I was inconsolable. It took months for me to come to terms with losing him, and many years before the tears stopped. I would try not to think about him as whenever I did, I always ended up in tears. I still think about him to this day, and it still makes me sad as he was such a wonderful baby and I know he would have been a fantastic little brother.

Thinking about Adam always brought back memories of Scotland. Although that was not the only bad thing to have happened to me at that young age, there was also, the 'affair' that my mother had.

It was not a pleasant period, but I knew that in the months leading up to our departure for brighter skies, my mother had been seeing a man from my father's workplace. He would sneak round to see her when my father was out or at work. Often I would find myself confined to the bedroom with my sister and brother, while she entertained her friend. I never understood why we had to stay out of the way, but we always conformed to my mother's demands. When I was a little older, I soon realised what she had been doing.

I remember the day that my father found out, he was furious and my parents had a huge argument. The yelling and shouting could be heard all the way down the street, we three children scuttled off to our rooms in order to avoid any fallout! A few days later, my father came home from work early and caught Keith at our house, he was in the living room with my mother. He went mad, driven by rage, jealousy and frustration, he grabbed his love rival by the shirt collar and hoisted the man out of the front door and shoved him, roughly, onto the sharp, gravel path. Keith quickly turned round and glowered at my father, I could see red marks on his face where my father's fist must have made contact. He scrambled to his feet and scurried off to his car, the tyres screeching as he quickly sped away. It was not long afterwards that we had planned the move to Rhodesia; my father's ultimatum to my mother was that she gives up her lover and the family moved together, or he would leave and be gone from our lives forever. He wanted to have a new start for all of us, as a family and I suspect that my mother did too.

So this was to be a new start for all of us, but would it be? There was so much we had left behind, friends, family, school and least of all Adam's grave. I would miss him; as I had often visited his grave on Sundays, as regular as clockwork. My mother and I would climb over an old stonewall, and run cross an open field, often with cattle feeding on the grass. Then we would hop over the low brick wall at the back of the cemetery. It was only a matter of a few yards to his grave, marked by its small marble headstone.

Looking back we had moved around a fair deal, and we had spent a year in the Isle of Man, just prior to the move to Bulawayo, but my best and clearest memories of living in Scotland are of a caravan that we had lived in for about a year. The caravan was based at a caravan park in a farming area of Ayrshire, near to a town called Stewarton.

It was our permanent home, spring, summer, autumn and winter—and in the winter it could be a very cold place indeed. It was not very big, but it had a bedroom, a large lounge with kitchen area and a bathroom. At the end of the lounge was a set of glass doors, similar to patio doors and they were always open in the summertime to let in the warmth of the sun. We three children slept in the bedroom, while my parents had a sofa bed in the lounge.

The bathroom did not have a proper toilet or a sink; in fact, it was just a small, empty room! We had a large, plastic, chemical toilet, which my father would regularly have to take away and empty, not a job that I would have enjoyed! Nonetheless, it had to be done. When the toilet began to get full; I hated to use it and would often prefer to wait until I got to school or a friend's place and used theirs instead. To me it was a foul smelling, overflowing vat of excrement, Yuk!

The bath was another thing too—it was an old tin bath, which mother would fill with boiling water. My mother had no sense of shame; she once left me sitting in the bath with the bathroom door wide open, while she answered a knock at the caravan door. It was a group of my friends, mostly boys, wanting me to play football. Well they only just caught a glimpse of me as I sank under the water to protect my (then eight-year-old) modesty. I felt so embarrassed; I swear I nearly died of shame.

It was cold in the winter yet it was also an exciting place to live. There were many times that my father would find me climbing the ruins of a derelict cottage nearby. He would haul me down from the rotting rafters time after time, telling me how dangerous it was, that I was never to do it again, but

I was a mischievous child and rarely heeded to what I was told.

I would sit up there for hours, watching the farmers at work, spying on my siblings, seeing what the neighbours were up to as well as hiding from my parents. There's always a bully no matter where you go, and this time, it was a large chubby boy, who was only a bully due to his size and the fact that he was three or four years older than the rest of the kids at the site. Plus, it did not help that his mother was the site caretaker. We all stayed out of his way but to be fair he never really bothered with me.

Lucy, Richard and I often went exploring the fields and streams near to us, catching frogs and small fish to keep in jars. I remember once putting a large jar of frogs-spawn under our caravan, it was soon forgotten, until my mother found it. Then I was severely reprimanded with a warning not to do it again. Mother had a temper and we were all wary of her for it, she would lash out for the simplest thing and often with whatever was in her hand, be it a shoe, hairbrush, belt or just a firm hand. She could leave you quaking in your boots with just a glance! Lucy always seemed to come off the worst. One thing I do remember very well was that Mother never ever hit Richard, as he was her blue-eyed boy.

I remember one bitterly cold, winter day when mother was shouting and yelling at Lucy. My mother had an extreme dislike for the Scottish accent; perhaps because she was from English parentage, but she wanted us to speak properly and regularly reprimanded and chastised us for any mispronunciation or use of slang. Today she was trying to get Lucy to say 'bird' but Lucy could not do it. She was only six, and had a strong accent, as we all did, with a typical Scottish burr about it, so when she said bird; it came out as 'burd'. She tried and tried, but she could not do it, eventually mother snapped, she accused her of deliberately not saying it properly, and smacked Lucy hard with the hairbrush she had in her hand. She hit her with such force that the handle snapped in two and went flying across the room. She banished Lucy outside to practice until she could say it properly, then and only then, would she be allowed back inside.

Lucy went outside crying, she was cold, sore and frightened. There was not much that I could do, but I wanted to help her. I was only eight myself and we were both afraid of our mother's temper. She was sitting on the concrete step which led up to the caravan door. She was crying, shaking, shivering from the cold and repeating 'burd, burd, burd' softly to herself. No matter how much she tried, or how many times she said it, she could not do it. I sat beside her, and I would say the word slowly, trying to get the vowel sounding just as it should and yet she still struggled. There was nothing to do, but to sit it out and wait until mother let her back inside. I chose to sit and wait with her.

We sat on that cold, hard step, for hours, until our bottoms were numb with the cold. Our hands were blue, our faces were frozen, and we could not feel our frozen red noses. At one point I noticed that Lucy's lips were blue.

'Your lips are blue Lucy', I said as I moved closer to her and we huddled together to keep warm.

Eventually mother let Lucy back inside and then went on to give me a roasting for having tried to help her! Lucy tried to apologise for not saying the word correctly. I remember her crying and sobbing as she said 'sorry mum' repeatedly.

My mother does not believe in saying sorry, she says it is a waste of time.

"Why would I say something that I do not mean?" is her reply when asked about it. Apparently she never did anything that she had not intend to do and therefore 'sorry' was irrelevant. So, because of her lack of consideration for others, she ignored Lucy's pleas.

I'm sorry was a regular phrase in our childhoods as my mother may not believe in it for herself, but she sure insisted that we said sorry every time she felt the need for us to.

Anyway, here we were, nearly two years later and this was to be a new beginning, at least I was hoping that here in this glorious warm sunshine, we would see less of mother's temper. My parents had been going through a rough spell in their marriage, perhaps this would prove to be their much-needed new beginning.

We very quickly moved into a house in the Queens Park East area of town, this was temporary, until we found somewhere more permanent. It was a nice house, with a large garden. There was a large tree close to the gate and I used to enjoy sitting underneath it, out of the extreme rays of the afternoon sun. On many an occasion, I would climb its lower branches and laze in the shade. The house had three bedrooms, a lounge, kitchen, and bathroom. Wow, a proper bathroom, with a proper toilet and proper bath!

There were also some servants' quarters to the back of the property. At the time of moving in there were plumbers just finishing off the showers in there. Well I can't tell you how long it had been since I had last had a shower, and I just couldn't see good showers go to waste, so I pleaded with mother to let us go and try them out.

"Please, please, please?" I begged.

Eventually, with the help of my ever curious and persuasive little brother, Richard, she relented. The three of us scuttled off to find soap and towels before heading to the showers. There were three of them and we wasted no time in getting all lathered up. We laughed and squealed under the warm water and played with the soapy bubbles for what seemed like hours. I would make handfuls of soapsuds and blow bubbles at Richard and Lucy, laughing as they dodged the big white clouds and they blew bubbles back at me as well as covering my head with so many suds that I looked like I had a cloud for a head, well that's what Richard thought I looked like. Richard tried to turn himself into Santa with a white beard and moustache made from suds; Lucy and I were almost hysterical with laughter just watching him trying to keep the soapy beard and moustache on his face. Each time he moved the suds would slide down his chin and he had to try again, and again, and again resulting in Lucy and I crying with laughter at him.

The front of our new house had a small, red stoep (porch). Its vibrant red colour was maintained through regular waxing with a soft cloth and lots of sweet smelling red wax. I often used to do the waxing; it was an enjoyable and very messy job, probably the very reason why I like it. I would brush the wax all over the floor with a hard bristled brush. To shine the wax I used soft cloths to buff the wax. After a while the whole area would be quite shiny and perfect for sliding on. So I would take a larger cloth and kneeling on it, I would slide across the floor. Sometimes Lucy and Richard would join in and we would race to see who could slide the furthest. It was a lot of fun for us and my mother had one less job to do.

As part of our settling in, my parents decided that we could have some pets, so we opted for a couple of dogs. We soon had a French poodle puppy called Monica and a slightly older Scottish terrier called Moira. We chose names according to their breed, hence a Scottish and French name. They were energetic bundles of joy, we loved them dearly and they went everywhere with us in the station wagon that my father had bought. At night, they would sleep underneath the car, warm and safe.

Monica had long gangly legs and was a clumsy puppy, often sliding on the polished floors and porch of our house. Moira was much more placid, but still fun to play with. They would have been dreadful watchdogs, unless being licked to death was an option.

That was, until the night that we decided to go to the drive-in and see the latest movie. We clambered into the car, as excited young children do, and waited for father to lock up the house and join us. He had already switched the engine on, to alert the dogs and give them time to get out of the way before he reversed out of the drive. As soon as he began to reverse, we knew there was a problem. There was suddenly a sharp, high piercing yelp, coming from under the car, followed by the feeling of a soft thud as we drove over something.

We leapt from the car, we three children were crying with fear. It was too late for Moira, she had been trapped under the back wheel of the car and had died instantly, and Monica had a broken leg and needed to be taken to the vet immediately. We buried Moira in the garden, at a quiet spot under one of the trees. She had her favourite toy with her and we said our own simple, short prayers over her small grave; sadness remained in the house for days as we adjusted to our loss.

It wasn't long after that, that we moved to Bellevue, an area on the other side of town, and although we moved again three times over the next four years, we stayed in the same general area, yet close enough to complete our primary education without further upheaval, something I was greatly satisfied with, having attended some 12 schools already.

It was just as we were planning this move, when mother told us her news. She was expecting a baby! Well, we had only been in the country for a few weeks and now there was to be a new addition to the family.

Indeed, it really did seem like a new beginning for all of us, and I remember being so happy to be living in a country of such beauty, with marvellous weather, and really friendly people. However, things were not all rosy as there was more upset to follow.

MY SCHOOL DAYS

A couple of weeks after moving in to our next new home, I started school. The school grounds were large and open, unlike any school I had ever seen in Scotland. There were playing fields all around and a huge car park with a bicycle shed to keep all our bikes safe. A great number of children rode their bikes to school, even little kids were safe to ride to school on their own or with siblings. I liked that, and vowed that I would get a bike and ride it to school with my friends, even though I lived less than ten minutes walk from school.

The school was all on one level, there were no stairs and the classrooms were bigger than in Scotland too. The rooms had very large windows, all along one full length of each room, looking out on to the field and track areas. This was very different to the small windows of previous schools in Scotland, which were usually so high up that it was impossible to see out of them and the little amount of sunlight that eventually managed to get through them was dismal.

Here things were brighter as the sun streamed in through the windows, and they were often left open to let cooling air into the warm classrooms.

I was taken into my new classroom and seated next to Penny, a pretty, young girl with bright blue eyes and long blonde hair. I was surprised that some of my new classmates seemed to recognise me, one boy came to me and asked if I was the girl from the front page of the newspapers. I was very happy to acknowledge that I was. I even asked him to bring in the paper for me to see, and when he did I was surprised. There I was, right in the middle of the front row! It was only then that I had actually seen the picture for myself. I felt like a movie star; well, for a day or two anyway. I was the new girl and everyone wanted to know me. That had never happened to me before and I like it. Children would follow me at playtime and sit in groups round me in the classroom; I had never received so much attention. Although the attention did not last very long, it did help me to make friends very quickly and I was soon at ease in my new surroundings.

My family had moved around a lot; as my father was always on the look out for that bigger, better job opportunity, especially if it meant more money. In fact we had moved so often that I had been to so many schools by this time, twelve of them in fact, that I no longer allowed myself to make close friends, because I was always on the move and would feel sad at losing yet another good friend. I did not isolate myself though and I had many friends to play with, I just did not become attached to any of them. At this school I felt different and I found that being the new girl was much easier than I had expected.

I made a few new friends, and I was very happy, especially when I spent time with my friend Penny. After we had been there for a few months I felt even more settled than ever. This time it felt as if we were here to stay, our new beginning was truly taking effect. I allowed myself to accept Penny as not only my best friend, but also someone that I began to trust and confide in.

A few months later my baby brother John was born. It was a warm Monday morning in late September. My father came into my bedroom and woke me at about 4:00 a.m., to tell me that the baby was coming and that he was going to take my mother to the hospital. He said he needed me to help him out and that I had to get up quickly, get washed and dressed into my school uniform. Then I was to make sure that Lucy and Richard were ready for school and that we had all eaten breakfast, before he returned from the hospital to take us to school.

I enjoyed primary school, although with a history of always being the new girl in the class; I had a tendency to bury my head in a book somewhere, but here in Africa, the schooling was different. We started much earlier in the day, usually very early, well before nine o'clock and we were out of school before 2 pm. That gave us the afternoon to enjoy the fantastic climate and best of all—to play! I went out on bike rides, went swimming with friends either at their pool or at the one we had at our house. We went exploring parks, and playing fields, played tennis and even went to the tennis club with Penny. She was my best friend at the time and would be for a few years. Life was never dull or boring as there was always something to do.

Most of my lessons were based on all things African; I had to learn all about the African culture, history and geography. Strangely, I became very interested in history and geography when they were focussing on Africa; previously I had had no interest at all in these subjects and would have daydreamed through much of the lesson. However, the customs and habits of the African tribes and their way of life was of extreme interest to me and I still have a fascination for some of these old cultures, and the knowledge that there are still isolated people in Africa who live according to these old teachings. I was particularly interested in the witchdoctor or shaman as they were known.

As much as my junior school days were filled with lots of fun and laughter there was terror as well! I have never known teachers like those in Africa!

An example of the 'rules' I experienced, was the implementation of punishments. Corporal punishment was very much the norm. Each morning we would have a mental arithmetic test and often this would be followed by a spelling test too. I usually got full marks in both of these, but for some reason, one morning I got an incorrect spelling and this meant that I had to take the 'punishment'. For this, I received six whacks of the ruler on my open palm. My hand was sore, red, inflamed and the pain was overwhelming. Everyone had a punishment that morning; I guess the words must have been too hard for the class as a group.

The following day, the same thing happened and I was yet again going to pay the penalty. This time was a little different instead of six slaps of the ruler; I was given the choice to have six 'dumps'. When I chose to have the dumps, I had no idea what was going to happen. My teacher closed his hand into a fist, with his middle finger raised slightly, so that the knuckle of that finger protruded above the rest. He then took my hand and pulled my arm straight, and proceeded to hit me sharply in the crease of my elbow joint. Wow, that was painful, I couldn't believe how much it hurt, he did that six times. After the punishments were handed out, we all sat at our desks, very quiet, subdued and one or two of the boys in the class were crying, they had been given more 'punishments' than the rest of us as they had failed on more answers. The teacher then informed us that we were not to tell our parents about what he had done.

Of course, that didn't happen, we all told out parents and the following morning the school was inundated with calls from our irate parents. The headmaster came into our classroom and inspected our arms. Many of us had visible bruising from the previous morning and he could easily see them. He left the room only to be followed a few moments later by our teacher. Sometime after that the teacher returned, collected his briefcase and a few things from his desk and prepared to leave. Just before he left the classroom, he turned towards us and in a horrible, threatening and angry manner, he said,

"I told you not to tell your parents, and now because some little wimp squeaked to mummy, I am out of a job."

I was startled at what he had said, suddenly I panicked, thinking that it was my mother who called the school. At the same time though, I was secretly thrilled to hear that he was leaving.

He had been the one who had treated me so badly on the climbing frame too. It was the most petrifying experience I ever had at school. It had started one Friday morning, when we had our Physical Education (PE) class on the field. There was a large climbing frame there, and we had to take turns to climb to the top, somersault over the top bar and climb down the other side. It was a simple flat frame, made from railings in the shape of a large square which contained smaller squares within it. There were sixteen squares in all, four squares wide by four squares high. Each square was wide enough for a person to climb onto and a short reach to the next. The only problem was that as the frame was open and poorly supported as it wobbled every time you got to the third railing or above it. Well, I have a morbid fear of heights, there was no way I would make it to the top never mind somersault that top bar! I tried though; I climbed as far as I could, reaching the third rail, and I slipped through the bars to the other side and climbed down. The teacher did not approve of that! He made me go back up repeatedly, but there was no way that I could go over that top bar. He left me feeling sick with fear at the end of the lesson, because he told me that on Monday I would do it properly!

I spent the entire weekend fretting about it and by Sunday night, I had the most awful stomach cramps, fear was taking hold of me. I told my mother that I was ill and would not be able to go to school the next day, but she sensed I was afraid of something and not ill, so she sent me to school. I wish she had asked me what the problem was; it would have been so much easier to be able to tell her. So the next morning I diligently went off to school, feeling scared, sick and petrified of what lay ahead of me.

As expected, we had PE in the field again, once more, he asked us to go up the climbing frame, and as usual, I was unable to do it. He barked at me to get up there, I tried, scrambling up the metal framework, but all that happened was that I managed to get myself up to the top bar and became firmly stuck! I was petrified and frozen with fear; afraid to look either up or down, I had nowhere to go but stay where I was. My friend Penny came up and slowly coaxed me down again.

'Come on, you can do it' she said, climbing up the frame to coax me down.

'I can't do it' I whispered, 'I'm so scared I can't let go of the bar.'

Within a blink of an eye, Penny had somersaulted over the top rail and was now on the other side and facing me. I looked at her with tears in my eyes, my hands were soaked with sweat and I was terrified of losing my grip and falling down. My knuckles were turning white as I gripped the railing and held on for dear life.

'Penny, please stay with me, I can't get down'

She replied, 'Okay, we will go down together.'

Steadily we climbed down the frame, at one point she shot ahead of me and I cried out to her to come back up.

'Don't go too fast, stay next to me please,' and so she returned and together we made the slow decent which was only a few feet, but it seemed like I was up the side of a mountain.

Once my feet hit the ground I let go of the railing and sank to the floor, my legs were like jelly and it took all my inner strength not to burst into tears. Well at least I had given it my best shot; I had never managed to get as high as I had done today, so in a small sense I felt that I had achieved something.

This became a regular torture event in my school days and I soon developed an intense dislike for PE and my teacher! I guess he must have thought that I would get over my fear of heights by persevering and pushing me to go further each time. Well he failed, as it did not work and I never made it over the top of that dreaded bar. But he was going now, so I was happy that I would not have to do it anymore.

This soon became one of the highlights of my school days. Soon after he left, Mr Edwards took over as my teacher, he was a lovely, wonderful, child-friendly man. He would sing Neil Diamond's 'Sweet Caroline' to me every day when I arrived at school. I soon became teacher's pet and I wasn't a bit bothered that I could be teased by my classmates. This was because he inspired all of us to do the best we could. I was able to create beautiful poems and limericks; often my work was displayed on the classroom walls. Obviously there was also work from my classmates as well, but I was always filled with pride when something of mine went up, in the past I never seemed to be able to produce the goods and my work was rarely displayed. If I had to choose my best school, best class, best teacher—the answer would always be the same, Mr Edward's lessons were always interesting. He never told me off for poor handwriting, although he did once ask why I had to write so fast—I guess that's why it's so sloppy, and I have never been able to slow down, no matter how hard I try.

I recall another day when I managed to persuade my parents to let me go to school on my bicycle. I was about eleven at the time and I had not long had my bike. It was much too big for me, but I loved it and was able to ride it really well. Braking was a problem as the saddle was very high up and as I pulled on the brakes and came to a stop I had to jump down from the saddle, or risk falling over to one side like a comic clown from some circus show. I often stopped with such a hard jolt, that when I landed on my feet, the pedals would scrape the back of my legs and leave grazes and bruises as the bike came to a clumsy halt. I even resorted to using my feet as brakes, as my hands were too small to reach across the wide handle bars and pull on the brake handles. My mother did not appreciate the wear and tear on my shoes.

On this particular day though, I arrived at school in plenty of time to show my bike to all of my friends. However, unknown to me there was to be a bicycle check by the local constabulary. I did not know that this was something that was undertaken each year, in order to check that all bikes were licensed and that the children rode a bike that was of an appropriate size to their height. Well, I was proud of my bike and it did not matter that it was too big for me. Therefore, when we were all asked to go and fetch our bikes and line up for the inspection, I did not hesitate. Off I trundled and fetched my pride and joy. I brought it to the back of the waiting queue and waited my turn.

I was not a happy bunny by the end of my turn with the inspector though! I was told, very clearly and sternly, that I was too small for the bike and that I was to push the bike home that afternoon and not ride it again until I had grown big enough for it. Even worse, I did not have a license and therefore could not ride it on the roads anyway! Well you could have knocked me over with a feather! I had no idea I had to have a licence for my bike, apparently my dad knew though! He soon sorted one out for me, they only cost about fifty cents at the time, and I was given a new, shiny, metal disc, which I had to attach to my front wheel axle. Each year these discs were issued in a different shape and colour, they were often proudly displayed as a fan shaped collection around the front wheels of most children's bikes. I was no exception and soon I had my own rainbow of colour as I built up my collection of licence discs.

One of the most prominent school memories I have, is being told off for my poor handwriting, I admit it was horrendous—a common phrase to describe my work was usually along the lines of 'Kay, your writing looks like a chicken has walked through ink!' Well, actually I would have said a spider would have been a better description, as it truly was awful. I would have to do handwriting practice for hours, writing row after row of Aa, then Bb, and Cc until I had perfected my letters. That was not the end of the problem though, I still had to put these perfect letters together and make beautiful words, which did not happen, no matter how much I tried. I just had to accept that I had dreadful handwriting and that was that. Although, my teachers did not see things like that and I still got plenty of handwriting practice given to me as part of my homework!

English was a good subject to learn at school, I enjoyed poetry and literature lessons. I often would have my work displayed on the work boards; it made me feel good about myself and helped build my confidence. I did exceptionally well through those last two years of junior school, finishing top of my class in my final year. I won a fantastic award for coming first in our year-end exams; it was a book token, which I received at our final assembly. I promptly went to the bookstore and chose a huge book of wildlife. My teacher gave me a copy of Tarka the Otter, which I still have to this day.

It was in January 1974 that I moved up to high school and it was an exciting time, although I had no idea how traumatic the experience would be. I was moving from a co-ed school to a girls' only high school. The boys' high school was next door to mine and I used to see many of the boys from my old classes on the way to and from school.

My first day at Montrose Girls High was filled with anticipation, I had my brand new uniform, a smart pale blue dress with white spots, accompanied by what can only be described as a wide brimmed floppy hat, although the brim of the hat was to be starched rigid. My dress was smoothly ironed and my hat's rim was perfectly starched, so that the brim provided an excellent sunshade for when I cycled there that on that warm, bright, sunny January morning. Having a beautifully starched hat was lovely, as long as it didn't rain, in which case it flopped down hanging in front of my eyes, giving me a hard time seeing the road ahead when I was on my bike.

When I arrived at school, I took my bicycle to the bike sheds, and found a secure place to keep it, making note of where it was. This bike shed was four times the size of my old school's and I did not want to forget where my bike was and then have to spend the afternoon looking for it, and no doubt feel foolish in the process. It did happen that I was unable to find my bike and then I would have to wait until most of the girls were gone, and then go round the almost empty shed and eventually find it. I swear sometimes it had been moved on purpose, I would often find it miles from where I would usually leave it.

Going to secondary school was a big step in my growing up, for a start the school was so far away that I had a huge responsibility to make sure that I got there on time. I sometimes had to ride like the wind if I had slept in. The big difference between primary and secondary school was that from now on it would be girls only! Also, I would have to get used to calling my teachers Miss or Sir, as all teachers were to be addressed in this way.

They say that children can be cruel to each other, particularly girls. Well, no one knows that better than someone who has spent any length of time with a group of girls, especially teenaged girls does!

After only a few days, it was clear that there were going to be problems in the classroom! With just short of thirty girls in my class there was bound to be problems. There were several girls who had joined together in groups to create their own cliques, one of these were the 'posh girls', those whose families had money. This group was lead by Debbie, a lovely blonde girl, who could be outspoken, but she was a fair person. They wore school uniforms like the rest of us, but one or two just seemed to look more glamorous. I found out later that they had their uniforms shaped with darts to enhance their figures, rather than have a straight tunic style dress, which to be fair was not very flattering at all. All they ever talked about was boys, boys, and boys! Oh yes, and how much money they spent that weekend, what music they had bought, or what elaborate or exorbitant plans they had for next weekend. They even planned their trips to the hairdressing salon together. Phew! What busy lives they had!

There was another group, there were about six girls who had all gone to junior school together, they stayed within their comfort zone and remained a clique of their own. They were a polite bunch and were friendly with everyone; they simply liked each other's company and spent their free time with one another.

I was one of the 'unfortunates' as I saw it—one of those who did not have a group, or clique, to join. That did not bother me, because to be honest, I just felt like that would mean committing to something, and I was not into commitment. Not at all! I did make friends with some other girls in the class, who were like me and felt that they did not quite fit in. I enjoyed my friendships with these girls as they made me feel like I had something to belong to, and yet at the same time, without asking more of me than I could give. For example, we would talk about our weekends, playing tennis, music and our after school activities, but there was no pressure on us to out-do each other, or be the best at whatever we were doing. We were simply having fun and told each other about it. Once or twice, we would meet up after school, but that was not something that any of my small group did much. This was mostly because we all lived so far apart from one another. The school covered an enormous catchment area so it was difficult for us to meet up.

During the school day, we would follow our timetables, as any school children would have done. We had all the usual lessons, maths, English, art, sciences, history and geography, but now we also had new subjects given to us. Among those in first year were French, Afrikaans and Needlework. I loved Afrikaans; I had already learned much of the language from living in South Africa for two years, when I was five or six. I was not fluent, but I could understand what was being said and provide appropriate responses. So I was very happy with the language and always did well, often I would get an A in tests and exams.

French lessons were awful! Not one single girl in my class was able to learn French with the teacher that we had. We felt like we were doing the same work, week in—week out. Some of the more confident girls, those from the 'posh girls' clique, made loud complaints in the lesson, to the teacher, however they were ignored! Things would only deteriorate though, as the teacher began to lose her patience and target specific individuals in the class, one of those was me! These were the days of the cane and other accepted forms of corporal punishment within schools. Our school favoured the cane and this teacher was not afraid to use it, even on us girls.

During each class, the French mistress, Miss Humphries, would shout, rant, rave and at times even scream at the class. I and a couple of other girls, was often on the receiving end of her abuse, which was not only verbal, but physical as well. She would throw her large wooden blackboard duster, or anything else that came to hand, at us! Chalk and rubbers were often flying through the air, although they just bounce as they hit you, but the wooden board dusters were a different matter. They would come flying across the room with a higher degree of accuracy and at a speed which left you unable to duck out of the way in time, landing on their mark leaving a bruise that would be visible for days. Occasionally a headshot would leave its victim with a shocked and often stunned feeling, which would temporarily throw off any concentration—obviously!

I had to remain focussed and get on with my work no matter what missiles would be heading out across the room. Everybody in class thought that woman was an evil witch, and the only teacher with whom we ever had a problem! By the time I left the education system, I would have gone to 16 different schools and yet this was the only teacher who ever really, and deeply, troubled me.

One day, Miss walked into the classroom with her usual long face and straight away she glowered at me. Sitting in my seat, third row back and second seat from the right, I just wanted to shrink away and disappear. I could feel the pit of my stomach churn as she gave us that heartless, cold stare. Why did I have to sit here, I felt like I was in the middle of the room and could not get away from her line of vision.

On this day, Debbie raised her hand and took an early opportunity in the lesson, to voice her disapproval at the way the class was progressing, or rather not progressing. She was unhappy that after all these months, none of the class felt like they were learning and we were unable to understand or converse in French. Debbie had friends in the lower classes and she said that our peers, were more adept at French than we were, and that was not only frustrating, but embarrassing. Well, that just opened a can of worms!

Miss Humphries snapped at Debbie and told her to stay quiet and get on with her work. Miss then issued us all with some written tasks and after only a few minutes decided to have us do some verbal phrases and/or terminology. Well, none of us had yet had the chance to revise the work we had just been given; many of us could hardly speak the language never mind understand what we were saying, and this was midway through the last term of the year!

Immediately, Miss pounced on me, asking me to recite something that was in the written task. As was custom in her class, I stood up to give my answer. Like the rest of the group, I had not managed to work that far into the tasks and so had no idea what she was talking about. I tried to tell her that I was still working on them and that I did not understand what she was asking of me, but she would not listen to me and went on to begin another verbal ear bashing. I had undergone this many, many times during the past ten or eleven months, but today it was too much and I was unable to let her scathing remarks wash over me. It did not take long before I could feel tears prickle at the back of my eyes. I looked round the classroom at my classmates for support; I knew I was not the only one still studying through the French work.

The whole class seemed to be watching me, as I stood there, a forlorn, quiet, petite and probably sad figure—suddenly a voiced boomed across the classroom. It was Debbie! I looked across to the back of the room to see her standing at her desk, she was quite a tall girl, with a generous build, and she seemed to take up the whole corner of the classroom with her size.

"Enough!" She shouted and demanded that Miss stop picking on me, she told her that she was aware that it had been happening all year long and that due to the lack of teaching and the way that I and some of my classmates were being treated, she announced that she was going to go on strike and would do no further work for the rest of the year. Then she dropped down into her seat, with an angry heavy thud.

The rest of the class were initially taken back and stayed quiet. I was still standing at my desk on the opposite side of the room from Debbie, but could feel that I needed to say something, so I commented on the fact that she was correct. I had to think carefully about what I was going to say. Two other girls, Irene and Dawn, and I already knew that we were being picked on and that we had been targeted as easy prey by the teacher. We had in the past, acknowledged between us, that it may have been due to the fact that all three of us were quiet, shy and fairly timid girls by nature. By the time I had thought it through and worked out an appropriate reply, the rest of the girls had taken in what was happening and had started to inform the teacher that they too were on strike. What? I came back to reality with a thump, what was happening now? A strike? What strike? Suddenly, I found myself supported by my peers; the French class was on strike! I could not quite fathom what was happening, as around me, one by one the girls, stood up and voiced their united front. The strike was on.

Miss Humphries was so angered and outraged, at the thought of her class being on strike, that she spun round and waltzed out of the room with her nose in the air and a loud bang, as the heavy, wooden door slammed behind her. What were we doing? Were we mad? How much trouble would we be in for this? Had I actually joined this strike too? Yes, I believe I had summoned the strength to add my voice to the growing numbers.

We all flopped down into our chairs and looked around the room, then we started to laugh, the whole thing seemed quite ludicrous really. I was bewildered about what we were doing yet at the same time, I was very happy about it.

A few minutes later, the door opened again and with a flounce in walked Miss, accompanied by our headmistress, Ms Bedford. Oh No! This was it; we were in trouble now, we sat in silence, as we awaited our fate. Ms Bedford began to speak, softly at first, then she began to raise her voice and told us she would not tolerate such behaviour in school, especially from young people such as we were. She went on to chastise us quite severely but at the same time, she did try to understand what had happened. We let Debbie take over in the explanation of what was going on. Although there was only one girl talking for most of the time, we were all right behind her. Indeed we were a united front.

By the end of the lesson, an agreement had been reached. There would be no further French lessons for our class for the rest of the year, which had only about six or seven weeks to go anyway. Within days, Miss Humphries was gone. We were all happy, fortunately for us, the following year we would only be doing one foreign language and we had all chosen Afrikaans. I think that was the only reason why we got away with what we did. Living in Africa, it made a lot of sense to learn an African language rather than French.

Looking back on that day, it was easily one of the worst schooldays that I had. I was humiliated, to the point of tears by my teacher, in front of my peers. BUT, at the same time, I found it a blessing, as I was freed from the torture of those lessons. Gone, were the mornings, waking up in fear of that class, unsure of what would happen today and no longer would I be wondering which one of us would be on the receiving end of her abuse. I think it felt good that something had been done, but why it had to take so long was beyond me, perhaps we were too shy to approach the teachers or talk to someone about it, I know I told my mum, but she never listened to me, or even believed what I said anyway, so it was pointless to look to her for help.

I think it was also apparent that there was something else there that day, in that the headmistress, so readily agreed to cancel our classes for the rest of the year. I feel that she must have known there were issues with that particular teacher and that our complaints were genuine. Years later I could look back at this and laugh, it was pretty funny really, worst still was the fact that nothing changed, lessons resumed as normally timetabled, the only difference was that we had another teacher.

It is often said that your school days are the happiest days of your life; well with me I'm afraid they were completely the opposite. I found myself on the receiving end of many a bully, despite my efforts to be friendly and accommodating. In later years, I attributed this to the fact that I was a very small for my age and being of a quiet disposition, I was an easy target. It would not have been any easier if I had had a target hung above my head, or a note round my neck saying 'Pick on me!'

My main bully at the girls' high school was a girl called Roberta. We started at the school together in our first year, by the middle of the second year she had turned into another evil witch! She used to be quite a quiet girl, with one or two close friends in the class and we were good friends at one point. She had the misfortune to have a spinal problem which meant that she had to have a lot of time off school at the beginning of our second year; by the middle of the year when she returned to class she had changed. If I remember correctly, she had an accident of some sort, which had damaged her neck and spine, the details of which I am unfamiliar.

Back in school now, her whole demeanour was different, she was no longer the happy and cheerful girl I once knew and she seemed to single me out from day one. She came in to class wearing a full head and back brace, supporting her fully from the top of her head all the way down to the bottom of her spine. The head brace was actually screwed to her skull. This meant that she was restricted in her movements and would be unable to take part in any form of sport or physical education (PE) classes. In our morning register session, we were asked to take care and ensure that we did not bump in to her and to try and provide her with the support she needed in getting from class to class, carry her books, open heavy doors, etc, as she would be unable to do much of that for some time.,

The whole brace thing seemed really harsh and uncomfortable and I'm sure it must have been horrendous for her to wear, nonetheless, that did not give her the right to target me as an outlet for her anger! I was not the only target, although at the time that did not matter to me. I felt as though she hated me the most, I suspect her other victims felt the same way.

Every time she passed me in the corridor or classroom, she would kick or hit me as she went by. Most often, she would slap me hard with her open hand or wooden ruler and laugh with her friends, my skin very quickly turning beetroot from the sheer force of the slap. On many an occasion, she would hit me on the head when we were passing on the stairs. I really felt that she enjoyed this the most and found it particularly entertaining, especially since she could hit me from a position of height. If it was a day where we had any sports, she would use her hockey stick or tennis racket to knock me on the top of my head. She would wait for me on the stairwell or landing between floors. As I would be coming up the stairs, she would be able to look down and see me coming, as soon as I was within reach she would lash out and hit me as hard as she could. She did this to several girls, but we all felt helpless to defend ourselves. That brace was a good deterrent and she knew it.

Break times and at the end of the school day were no different, she would find one of us and take whatever pleasure she could in ridiculing or bullying in whatever way she could. Despite my questioning why she would hit/push/slap and humiliate me, I never once received an answer.

I told my parents about this, but the only solution I was given, was that I had to fight back. How do you do that when someone is in a full body (back and neck) brace, which is screwed to his or her head? I am not sure what I expected them to do to help me, but I found their lack of support distressing. After months and months of this, I began to despise school even more than I already did and would feign illness to avoid going. I became rather good at that and after some time I realised that it was not getting me anywhere as I still had to go and she would still be there, waiting on me, when I did.

One day several months on, I saw her come into school without her brace, seeing her without it was almost as shocking as when I first saw her with it. I was pleased that at last she seemed to be healing and hoped that this would signal the end of her bullying. I had felt certain that it was the stress or strain of wearing the brace that made her so aggressive.

Later that morning when I was on my way to art class, we met in the stairwell. She stood there in the corner, chatting to two of her cronies, and I walked quietly past them. I had not seen her standing behind them, so it took me by surprise when she reached out and grabbed me by the arm. I spun round to see who it was and was instantly met by a fierce stinging on my arm. It was then that I realised that she had twisted my wrist so sharply that she had twisted it backwards and caused a sharp pain to shoot through my arm and hand. I withdrew my arm swiftly and began to turn away to leave the stairwell, when her ruler caught the side of my face.

I could feel the anger rise from deep within me, as I turned towards Roberta, tears in my eyes, I stared at her. I was furious, angry, hurt and upset. I had taken this for so long and now I was at breaking point. It had been well over a year since all this had begun and I had had enough!

I do not know where I found the courage from, but I dug deep down in my soul and found the strength to give that girl the hardest slap I could muster. I shouted at her and told her to leave me alone and find someone else to pick on, "enough is enough", I shouted. Taken by surprise her friends had backed into the opposite corner of the stairwell and so she was left alone with me. I glared at her as I bent down to pick up my dropped schoolbooks from the floor, and went off to my art class.

Surprisingly, that was the last time she did anything like that to me. I guess the surprise of me being able to fight back was enough to stop her. For me, it was a blessed release after months and months of frustration at not being able to defend myself. Without her protective brace to shield herself with, I finally felt able to give her what she deserved—a real good old fashioned slap!

It was around this time that I was to really feel the effects of my family's lack of finances. Schooling in Rhodesia was not free and there were school fees to be paid for each child each term, since there were three of us in school my parents had three sets of school fees to come up with. My brother, Richard, went to a school for children with special needs, as he was epileptic and had co-ordination problems due to being left-handed. Add to that the cost of uniforms and sports equipment, it was an expensive time for my parents. Any spare money always went Richard's way.

Being the eldest child, I often felt left out of things, and this time period was no exception. I had an old, battered tennis racket which I had bought for ten cents at a second hand store; this is what I used for tennis lessons. My white tennis plimsolls were so worn, that there were holes though the layers of the rubber soles. I had worn the same shoes for almost two years and they were worn out, but there was no money to have them replaced and they were well beyond the point of repair. This was often cause for great ridicule and teasing from the other girls, I don't think there was another girl in school in the same situation as I was, at least not until my sister started school two years after I did.

My teachers were completely unsympathetic and held me with contempt in my worn out uniform, tatty sports equipment and a general lack of financial contributions.

I had worn the same two tunic dresses since I started school and we were now half way through my third year! When I started at the high school, my mother had deliberately bought me dresses that were a couple of sizes bigger than I needed, in order to get more wear out of them and so she had been able to take up a large hem on each dress. Each year she would let down another few centimetres from the hem, this resulted in unsightly bands of colour around the bottom of my dress each time she did it. I only had these two dresses and the colour was fading when they were washed each week. They were also wearing very, very thin, but I was unaware of that—yet!

Apart from those two dresses, everything I had came from a second hand uniform shop that the school ran from an old classroom. I never had a coat or jacket and would cycle to school in the winter, in my uniform protected by a navy cardigan. A school blazer was something that I dreamed of but never owned, the nearest I came to it was an old plastic raincoat that I kept in my school bag.

A regular event during the school year was the dress length inspection. This was something that I had grown to dread, as each year passed and I failed the inspection another inch or so would be let down from the ever shrinking hem. Oh the shame and embarrassment of each new, visible, band of hem. Oh, how I hated these inspections!

Each inspection took place in the school hall, up on the stage. Each class of girls would parade into the hall, form a single line across the front of the stage and then kneel along the edge. The headmistress, or sometimes the gym mistress, would then come along and measure the distance from the wooden stage floor to the hem of each girl's dress. Any girl whose hem was more than ten centimetres above the knee was informed that her dress was too short and that it was to be lengthened or replaced. My skirt was often on the short side.

One day my dress could take it no more, and the back of it ripped and hung down like shreds of bandages. It had happened while I was sitting in morning assembly. The whole school would be crushed into the main hall, girls sitting in rows, crossed legged on the floor. As I rose to leave, my dress ripped open, it was so flimsy that I did not even feel the fabric tear. When I realised what had happened I burst into tears. My first thoughts were that mother would be mad at me, and then I wandered how would we be able to afford buying a new dress for me.

Wearing my only remaining dress, I arrived at school the next day, to a pleasant surprise from my classmates. All my fears left me in one glorious moment. As I approached my desk, two girls came up to me and they each gave me two dresses. The girls were from two of the cliques in the class and I had not had much to do with them, they meant well and I was overwhelmed with their kindness. I was usually the victim of their meagre jokes, but today they showed me that they actually cared about me. It was at that moment, I realised that my class of girls was one big family, albeit a difficult one at times, but we all looked out for each other.

I am sure that the entire class knew that I came from a family that had a small income and that it had a long way to stretch. During my time at high school, I had many problems with money. I was unable to pay the 20 cents needed for sewing lessons. This was a small charge to cover the cost of the materials, pins & needles and the upkeep of the sewing machines. My father said that there was no way that he would pay for it, I was tempted to use my pocket money, but my father refused to allow it. He decided he was going to write a letter to the headmistress. He informed her that as I was 'neither a thief nor a vandal' he would not be paying the 20 cents. I was horrified and ashamed of what he had done, I did not want to cause any trouble and I was uneasy at school over the next few days.

A week or so later, I was called into the headmistresses office, where I was told about the letter and its contents. Ms Bedford informed me that as I was unable to produce the required costs of maintaining the sewing machines, I was to be taught the art of hand stitching and embroidery. In reality, I never did any embroidery in needlework classes, but I did make skirts, aprons and other garments, all stitched by hand while the other girls whizzed along with the sewing machines. I had to do a lot of work at home, just to keep up with the class each week.

I had many occasions like these, all to do with a lack of money. I had problems with my sports classes as I did not have the required equipment. Netball, tennis and hockey sessions were the worst, as they were all outdoor activities and that meant I had to use certain sports equipment and wear plimsolls. My plimsolls were so old and worn out that not only was the sole flapping off like an old worn out tongue, there were holes right through the bottom which made my feet hurt when I ran in them. I was always the laughing stock when I wore them. I did not have a tennis racket or hockey stick either, so I was always threatened with detention for not having the required equipment for sport sessions.

One way of getting round this was to try and buy the items myself. This was an almost impossible task. At the time I was getting 50 cents a week pocket money and the cost of new sports equipment was extremely high. So, I came up with a plan to visit a local junk shop and see what I could find there. After a few weeks I found a tennis racket and handed over my two dollars. Hooray! I had a tennis racket. Well for a while at least, it was old, the wooden frame was weak in parts and after a few months it split and ended up in the bin.

I never did manage to get a hockey stick, and to this day I still have no idea how to play hockey as I never had the opportunity to take part and learn how to play the game. There were many tears over sports lessons and any other lesson that required any kind of financial contribution from my parents.

So you see, when I said I hated my school days it really is a gross understatement; I detested them with a vengeance. People would comment that your school days are often reflected on as the best days of your life, when you were young and carefree. When I left school there was no way that I was ever going to miss my school days, and to this day, I still do not.

Oh, do not get me wrong; there were good times, but not many of them. I enjoyed taking part in the school plays, always minor parts due to my shyness, but I liked to participate. I was an angel in one performance, which meant that my mother had to create an angel costume for me, from an old white sheet. The school had provided instructions in how to make one, but my mother had to do it her way. On the day of the dress rehearsal, I found myself in a pickle trying to get the costume on. One of the teachers came over to try and help me and she put the dress over me and I ended up with the dress down my front and the angel wings at my back—but nothing actually covering my prepubescent body! I was fourteen and mortified!

I was so small and petite that I had still not reached the stage where I could wear a bra. I was the only girl in the class who had yet to develop breasts. I was not yet having periods either, so I felt isolated and disconnected from the rest of the girls. A year later on and I was able to wear a bra, now I felt better! Now I felt like I belonged with my peers.

Penny and I would spend our breaks together, we were in different classes now, but we always rode to and from school together. Often on the way home we would sing our heads off, not worried about who heard us. I'm sure we sounded awful but we did not care, we were happy. It was towards the end of my second year of high school that I became aware that there was something not quite right with Penny and our friendship. She was often missing from school, if she went she would be late and then at the end of the day she dashed home before you could blink. I wondered if she had a boyfriend or something, but the reason was a much bigger problem. My friend had indeed acquired a new boyfriend, and he was much older, he was around twenty-two while she was a mere fourteen. Her parents knew nothing of him and I was sworn to secrecy. She would often be unavailable to go swimming or to play tennis, or catch up with other friends, as she was seeing 'him'. I never got to know his name, but I did know he was bad news.

At first it was hard to work out what was going on, but then Penny confided in me that she was drinking a lot at weekends while she was with him. She seemed to think that it was a harmless thing to do, yet she could not remember what had happened afterwards. I thought she was very daring and after each weekend she would have tales to tell us about her weekend, well what she could remember at least. After a while this began to worry me, she seemed to be spending less and less time at school and with me and our friends. The more time she spent with her boyfriend, the more distant she became to us.

I admit that I shed a few tears at school, usually alone in the toilets, where I would lock myself in a cubicle during break. I felt unable to talk to many people about how I felt and gain advice on what to do. I did manage to talk to my English teacher, Mrs Moore, who was very kind and considerate. She had noticed that I was subdued and after much prodding, she was able to get me to open up to her. She told me that whatever I said to her would be kept in confidence and only between the two of us. She reassured me that I would be fine, that I would survive school and become a much loved and admired adult. She listened to me as I poured my heart out to her about how I felt, the struggles I had without equipment, no money, being bullied and just life in general. My fourteen-year-old brain was in overdrive; I had tolerated almost three years of ridicule and hardship, now I felt I was at breaking point. Mrs Moore was a fantastic listener; she gave me all the time I needed to spill it all out. When I was done, she gave me a big hug and a few well-chosen words. Finally she told me, "All good things come in small packages".

From that day on, I have often reflected on her words, usually if I was feeling down or in a difficult situation, they have kept me strong and over the years, I have thanked her in my mind several times.

REALITY SETS IN

I was very quickly aware that here, in this new country, there were many, many more black people and with much darker skin, than back in Scotland. There were young, black children everywhere, they call black children pikinins in Africa. I often wanted to go and play with them but my parents would not allow me to. None of us were encouraged to mix with black people at all. It was 'not the done thing' and I soon began to learn that things were very different here, in my beautiful new home.

I had noticed that when I was on the bus with my mother going into town that the white people sat apart from the black people. I did not realise at first that this was how things were across the country, always apart, no mixing or socialising between races. This was called Apartheid, and I was going to have to get used to it. When we went swimming to the local pool, it was for whites only. Going to the cinema, was for whites only, the same for tennis clubs and schools. Everywhere you looked there were signs that said 'Whites Only'.

At school, we were taught the history of Africa and about the many tribes who had lived there. From the Kikuyu, Hutu, Swahili, Tutsi, Hottentot, Ndebele, Maasai, Zulu, Xhosa, Shona and even the Bushmen and Pygmy tribes. I'm sure that there were others, too numerous to mention, but we were taught about how the tribes had migrated from the north of Africa, travelling south, fighting for both land and survival. We also learned about Cecil John Rhodes and David Livingstone, famous white men, who forged through Africa, making their mark on the continent. I also remember studying the life of Ceteswayo and Shaka Zulu, which I found fascinating. Shaka, also known as Chaka, was well known for the calibre of his warrior armies, known as impes. The men he trained were very tough and disciplined. During their training Shaka would make his warriors danced on devil thorns to toughen their feet. Devil thorns are called that due to their size, they are a around 2-3 inches long and impossibly sharp. These warriors could easily run twenty miles a day, can you imagine being able to that? Ceteswayo is often referred to as the last great Zulu King. The amazing thing was, that even after teaching us how these lands had come about, and that it was ours, it belonged to the whites, not the black people who had fought for years to keep it as theirs. I never once questioned whether this was right or not—at least not until much later. All through my school years, I was indoctrinated with the rights and wrongs of our society, what was acceptable and what was not. Having black friends was not acceptable. Having a relationship with a black person was the ultimate taboo, mixed marriages were not acceptable and indeed they were not legally possible at that time either-.

I remember vividly the day that my geography teacher told us about her recent trip to the capital city, Salisbury, now known as Harare. There she had been immensely disgusted and appalled at the behaviour of a young, blonde woman, hanging on the arm of a black man. She described to us, how the couple had cuddled and kissed in public, then gave us the most severe warning that such behaviour in public or otherwise, would not be tolerated! We had it drummed into us every day that we were only to mix with our own kind, nothing else would be acceptable. She made it very clear to us that there would be no cavorting with a black man for any of us, heaven forbid! The sad thing is that at the time I felt as appalled as all the others, it was only later that I realised that it was not wrong at all and that it was quite natural.

I still remember the feeling of horror and disbelief of what she had told us. There was no way that my teenage mind could comprehend what she had said. My thoughts were wild and my imagination reeked havoc with my brain for the next few days. What had that blonde girl been thinking? How on earth did she do it, or even more so, why did she do it? How could she kiss a black man? Phew, that was something that I could not imagine without feeling repulsed. It was a topic that the girls in my class would discuss over and over. Now, I look back in horror at how I was raised, in reality, there is no shame in being with someone of another race, it's all about personal choice. Living in southern Africa in the early 1970s did not allow much 'choice' when it came to such things.

Penny and I delighted in taking on the subject, as a source of ridicule. We did not know any better, but now when I look back, I shiver at the thought of such hostile, negative and intolerant thoughts. This is how we were brought up and it seemed perfectly natural, until someone else pointed out that actually, it is nowhere near natural and certainly not acceptable in today's world.

In order to maintain this Apartheid, there were some extreme measures taken. Shopping was an unpleasant experience, black women would push and shove to get to the front of a queue, barter and haggle for the best prices, their loud, brash voices could be heard all around the town. White women were very different with their orderly queuing, and their quiet, discreet and generally polite habits. White women NEVER pushed and shoved to the front of the queue, but would patiently wait their turn to be served. They also tended to buy their items at the store without quibbling over the price, and they were never known to raise their voices as black women did. If a white woman was to raise their voice in public she would generally be described as a 'fishwife' an unpleasant and derogatory term, so most women were quietly spoken, implying politeness and being lady-like.

Each weekend, my parents would take us to play in Centenary Park in the centre of Bulawayo. We had to make sure that if any of us children needed the toilet, that we went to the 'White's only toilets', if we wanted an ice-cream from the small shop, we went to the main service window, around the side was a smaller window where black people would be served. This sort of thing was not uncommon and happened all over the country in a million and one ways. No matter what the activity or need, blacks and whites had to be kept apart. We had our own schools, dentists and doctors. We did not eat in the same restaurants and black people were not to be found in the white's only hotels, unless they were working there!

Well, there was a little bit of a rebel in me right from the beginning, and soon I had a black friend. Her name was Faith and she lived near us, in the servants' quarters at the back of the house where she worked. She was employed as a maid and had to keep house and care for the teenage child who lived there. Ironic that she should be employed for such a job, when she in fact was only fifteen when I first met her. The same age as the girl she was to care for!

I used to pop over to see her when it was quiet so that I would not be seen, sneaking behind the house to where she lived. It was a small building, comprising of a main living area, bathroom which had a toilet and shower, and another very small room where she kept her bike. She used to cycle to her home village to see her family at weekends, she often spoke fondly of them.

I used to enjoy listening to her talking about her life, where she grew up and what she wanted from life. I was very surprised that she felt she had all that she wanted. I guess, that's because of the way we are raised, she was brought up in the belief that black people served white people, and if you were lucky you would get a job like hers, where servants quarters were available. Not long afterwards, her brother was employed as a gardener for the same family. He was only a year or so older than she was and I was amazed at how hard they worked, and on reflection, how little they were paid for all their efforts. Sadly, our friendship was doomed from the start. It became harder and harder for me to see Faith, as I grew older and had more and more studying to do, I had less opportunity to go and see her. She was always a friendly and pleasant young woman, who I admired greatly and she was never upset or offended that I no longer visited as often as I did. She understood the difficulties as much as I did. Whenever we bumped into each other we were always friendly and warm towards one another and had a quick chat whenever we could. When it came time for me to leave Rhodesia, she was very unhappy, she felt that the country would not be able to survive without the structure and governing that the white people had created and maintained, despite the Apartheid.

One of the hardest things to come to terms with was the fighting that was going on. There were many times that I heard of friends who had lost fathers, uncles and older brothers. I had not been in Bulawayo very long when I realised that the country was undergoing considerable upheaval and that the guerrillas people were referring to were actually people and not gorillas! In my young, naïve ten-year-old mind, I had found it difficult to distinguish between the two, and it was only when I asked my dad, "what is a gorilla?" that I found out the truth. As I grew older I realised how ruthless these terrorists were, as they killed without mercy. Brandishing their weapons and killing anyone who did not share in their beliefs or activities, or perhaps got in their way was sickening. They were slaughtering not only white people at every chance, but also decimating rural villages, killing everyone in sight. The killing of black women, children and elderly people really scared me; in my eyes they were effectively killing their own people

The realisation that there was a real war going on and not just some daft bush fight scared the living daylights out of me!

As I got older and the situation was worsening the effects of the brutal fighting began to take place and strong changes were brought into school. While still in junior school I was not really affected by the fighting or 'the troubles' as my mother preferred to call it.

By the time I went to secondary school, in 1974, things were really beginning to change. My first year there was like any other would have been for many first year pupils, but girls were beginning to pair up (using the 'buddy' system) and cycle to school with a friend. Penny and I were inseparable, we went everywhere together, and safety in numbers was our motto.

No longer did we take shortcuts through the bush if we were on our own. If the streets were quiet, then even with a friend, it was safer to take the long route home and cycle through the streets instead of taking any short cuts, which could prove, risky or hazardous. It was very common to large groups of girls cycling to school together.

Each term had its share of fire drills, which were usually welcome breaks in studying. Since the weather was rarely unpleasant, the chance to be out in the sun for a few minutes rather than sitting at a desk was often accepted with open arms.

During my second year there, we were introduced to something called 'bomb' drill, this was closely followed by a similar 'terrorist' drill. These drills were essential for our well-being and safety. The bomb drill was quite simple, the school would evacuate in a similar way as for a fire drill, but we would meet as far from the buildings or cars as possible, so we were told to meet on the playing fields.

For the terrorist drill, all staff and pupils would gather in the main hall where a register would be taken and our parents would be contacted to come and take us home. The first time we undertook either of these drills was quite frightening, but we soon adjusted to them and they became as common place to us as routine fire drills were.

It was when I was about thirteen that I began to really become aware of the long term effects of the fighting. There were already good systems in place foe keeping safe and neighbourhood watches were organised in most suburbs. My father was involved with the watch in our area and routinely went out on patrol with other fathers. Usually they went out in small groups, pairs at an absolute minimum. They would stop and check any black people they came across, asking for their documentation and proof of identity. There was a curfew in place at the time, so anyone out at night was usually treated with suspicion.

Some months later, my father had to move to a place called Wankie, where he had a job working in a coal mine. It was about 300 miles from where we lived and my parents had ruled against moving there as it was close to the Zambian border. So, my father would go away for weeks at a time and come home to see us as often as he could.

It was only possible for us to go and see my father in Wankie a couple of times. We once went for three weeks during school time, and so I was issued with work to do while I was there from my teachers, so for me, lessons continued undisrupted. The first time that we went to see my father; we stayed in a caravan near to where my father's digs were. It was quite an adventure seeing him and exploring the surrounding bush and towns.

On our next stay, we went to visit the Victoria Falls and Wankie Game Reserve. This time we were able to live in a house not far from the coal mine and also the local shops. It was exciting and the weather was hot, humid and brilliant sunshine every day. The only downside was that the water we had to drink came directly from a borehole in the back yard and it tasted of lime. It was so strong it tainted everything that it touched. The only way that you could drink it, was when it had been kept in the fridge, at least when it was cold, the taste was almost bearable.

My father was working throughout our stay, and at one point he had to work night shifts for a few nights. We had all been warned that the area was a bit isolated and that we had to be careful at night. We had to ensure that everything was locked up and secure before we went to bed.

One evening, shortly after father went to work, my sister Lucy was looking out the lounge window towards the back garden. The grass was extremely long and was probably waist high to me. There was no real garden to speak of as the bush seemed to creep right up to the edge of the back path. Suddenly, she jumped up and yelled that she had seen someone in the grass. Instantly, my mother hit panic mode. She called all four of us children into the lounge where she could see us. John was only a young child of about three or so and he had no idea what was happening.

We sat there for some time before mother decided it would be best if we all went to bed. So off we went to our bedrooms, Lucy and myself in one room, Richard and John in another room, while our parents had the biggest bedroom. Not long after I had gone to bed, I heard my mother calling me, so I went to find out what was wrong. I got to her bedroom in time to help her push a single bed against the far wall of the room. What on earth was going on? Well, it seemed that she still felt that there was a 'presence' around the house and had decided that we should all sleep in the same room. So she had Richard to help her bring his bed onto her room and then we went to fetch my bed too. By the end of the evening there was a double bed and two single beds in her bedroom. My bed was placed firmly against the bedroom door to stop anyone from breaking into the room from inside the house. Mother had her bed across the French doors, to deter anyone from getting in from the outside. It was a free for all as to where you could sleep. I tried to sleep in my bed, but I was restless and haunted by images of being shot through the door, by some masked intruder! Therefore, I ended up on the double bed as well. I hardly slept a wink that night; the fear was crippling and kept me alert for most of the night.

The next morning, the beds were returned to their rooms and everything went on as normal, just like nothing had ever happened. Not a word was mentioned about it, and I do not believe that my father was ever told of my mother's folly of the previous night.

It was during this time that my father decided that I should learn how to shoot a rifle. We had one in the house for our safety and although my mother was familiar with it, he wanted me to know as well, just in case we ever needed to use it to defend ourselves. Therefore, he fetched his rifle and passed it to me. It was a monster of a gun. It was long, heavy and extremely awkward for me to manoeuvre. After showing me how it worked and how to load the bullets, and remove the safety, he then tried to show me how to hold it. He wanted me to be able to hold it correctly or the recoil was likely to break my shoulder or collarbone. I could not lift the rifle up. I was a slight, wisp of a girl, and the rifle was probably close to my height in length. Finally, I managed to raise the weapon, by resting the end of the barrel on the window ledge and then raising the butt of the gun to my shoulder. Heaven help me if ever we were in a situation, which called for me to use this thing! I worried and fretted for weeks afterwards.

My sister had a friend at school, her name was Tanya, she came from a lovely family, and she had a sister and brother as well as great parents. Her Dad was a wonderful man and I admired him very much, he always made me laugh whenever I went to visit them. There was a lot of love in that family, and as a father, it was obvious that he loved his children very much, he spent all his time with them and whenever I was there, he always joined in to play games and constantly kept us entertained. I remember being completely devastated at the news that he had been killed while serving with the army. He and a colleague had been blown up in his jeep, by a landmine. I had known he had been called up for national service and was dreading the time when my father would also be called upon to defend the country.

I cried bitterly at the loss, it all seemed so unfair. Penny was a great comfort to me at this time; she listened to my fears and understood why I was worried. Although Penny's parents were considerably older than most parents were, she had two brothers who would have to complete their national service too, and she feared losing one or both of them to the war. There was a three 'call up' rule at the time. Anyone who is drafted to join the army can be given a six month reprieve if their company felt that it was important for them to keep that worker during that period. This could only be done twice, on the third call up the men had to undertake their army duties.

Initially it was only Rhodesians who were drafted into the army, and as the need for men grew, the age range of draftees rose accordingly. The government then realised that they needed more people than they had available to them, so they brought in conscription for non-Rhodesians, this meant that all male children living in the country would have to complete their national service when they reached the age of eighteen. After that, they could be drafted to serve with the army at any given time in the future.

As the war progressed, even this was extended and all men below the age of thirty-five were called upon. This now included my father at that time. Fortunately, where he was employed felt that they would not be able to manage in his absence and they were able to get a six-month reprieve for him. We were all frightened and I was upset at the thought that he would not be coming back to us if he went. There were nightly news broadcasts telling of the deaths that day and how many men were shot or blown up by landmines. I did not want my father to become another statistic. Fortunately for us, or so we thought, my father would turn thirty-five soon and would then be too old to be called up.

A few months later though, he was called up again, the age of draftees had been raised to all men under the age of forty-five. Once more his company came to his aid and he was given another reprieve. It was at this point that the decision to leave the country was made. We would need to act swiftly and in secret, otherwise my father could have been charged as a deserter.

I was petrified now, the war was affecting my family directly and fear gripped me at night, I slept fitfully for months. At school, light-hearted banter about killing terrorists was replaced with real fear and concern for friends and their families. One day in the classroom, myself and a few of the girls even joked about walking through the bush, as gun-toting, bikini-clad bait to lure the terrorists from their hideouts, only to be shot by us and additional snipers as they appeared. A very unrealistic plan, but then we were only fourteen and fifteen year old girls, who did not really understand what all the fighting was about in the first place, and just wanted it all to end.

Factions such as the African National Congress (ANC) were all gaining strength in numbers. There were many African leaders across the continent that were dictators and were in some way, role models for the guerrillas, i.e. Idi Amin, among others. Even Robert Mugabe was feared at one point, despite being chosen to lead the country and had a hand in changing the country's name from Rhodesia to Zimbabwe.

SCHOOL GIRL ANTICS

When I was about fourteen, I began to spend more and more time at my friend Penny's house, sleeping over almost every weekend. We would sit for hours in her bedroom, listening to music on the radio and singing along to the hits of the day. Penny was the youngest of a big family and her bedroom reflected this, as it was a huge room with three single beds, for her and two older sisters, who had both recently left home.

One of our favourite songs to sing and dance to was the Elton John/Kiki Dee hit, Don't Go Breaking My Heart. We would each take a vocal and sing at the top of our voices, usually I was Kiki Dee. Singing in the bedroom, hairbrush microphones in our hands, and bouncing on the beds as we sang. We loved it, and one day, we promised each other, we would be stars!

Penny's mother was what I would call, a bit of a nutcase. Once when Penny and I had been out on our bikes, we had been almost half an hour late in returning, her mother went ballistic! She demanded that I apologise to her for the inconvenience I had caused. Of course, I apologised, after all, we were both late and therefore we were both at fault. However, she was not happy with a simple apology and as I crossed the lounge to go home, she lunged at me with a bread knife in her hand. She hit me hard, across the centre of my back, with the flat edge of the blade. I was certain she was going to stab me and I would die at the hands of the evil old woman. Penny shouted at her mother and told her to behave; the old woman immediately stopped what she was doing and went off into the kitchen, muttering to herself as she went. What a nightmare! I was always wary of Penny's mother after that.

There was a lot of unrest and regular disturbances in the area, mostly because of the fighting with the terrorists and because of this, I was forbidden to travel far from home. This meant that I always had to let my mother know where I was going and when I would be back because safety was a big issue during those times, we all had to be careful. Timing was essential, whatever time you set to be somewhere, you had to stick to it or people would worry and panic that something had happened to you.

And it wasn't only the black people who were a danger to us, only a few weeks earlier, a middle aged, drunken man had tried to drag my sister, Lucy, from her bike and into his car. She screamed loudly and I ran to her aid. Although she was only twelve and of slight build, she had, a good set of lungs and surprised her attacker with a massive, ear-shattering scream. I grabbed hold of Lucy's arm and pulled her towards me. Fortunately, the man was extremely drunk, his bloodshot eyes, glared at me, as I pulled her to safety. He sped off in his little battered, yellow Austin and we ran home to tell our mother what had happened. We were both shaken and tearful, but by the next day, we had put the episode behind us and were back out on the streets and playing with our friends and our bikes, as if nothing had happened.

As I have already mentioned, most weekends I would sleep over at Penny's house. I loved it, she was the youngest of fourteen children and the only one still at home, her parents were both elderly and Penny had been a very, very late baby indeed. There was something like twenty-six years between her and her oldest sister. There were twelve girls and two boys in total; I was amazed that anyone could have that many children. I was also surprised to see that her parents had a beach buggy as their family car. These cars were very popular in the 70s and early 80s, but usually with much younger people. I would try to stifle a giggle whenever I saw Penny's mother trying to get in or out of the car. They were not the most lady-like of vehicles for a chubby, much older woman to be climbing in and out of and so I always found it particularly amusing to watch.

Most Saturdays would be spent in Penny's kitchen, baking. We would bake scones, biscuits and cakes, storing them in airtight containers to try and prolong their shelf life. It was not unusual for us to find mouldy cake from the previous weekend still in the containers. While our efforts were in the oven, it was my job to clean out the containers of last week's crumbs, ready for the new batch, while Penny washed up after us.

Once we had finished with the baking, we would bask in the sun, sipping cold, clear, fresh water from the borehole in Penny's yard. It was the coolest, freshest, tastiest water I have ever had.

Sipping the cool drink, we would often sit in the branches of a huge, gnarly old tree at the far side of the garden. This particular day was no different to any other, and after our cakes were baked and on a rack to cool, we made our way across the yard to 'our tree'. We could sit up there for hours unseen, hidden by the huge leafy branches, watching people as they went about their business, unaware that they were being watched by two sets of curious eyes.

One day, we were sitting on the branch, like many times before, laughing at some old joke that Penny had made, when there was an awkward lurching of the branch. We heard a loud cracking sound and then there followed a sudden drop and we tumbled to the ground. Our tree had let us down, literally, the branch had broken off. We sat on the ground, both stunned and recovering from the jolt of hitting dry earth so rapidly. The branch had broken free from the rest of the tree and now there was a large split in the tree trunk where it used to be. Stunned, we looked at each other and tried to make some sense of what had happened, we had been sitting on this old branch for years, without the slightest hint that it was weakening. We mourned the loss of that branch as if we had lost a dear friend. We then found ourselves lost for a 'hidey-hole' to escape to, away from adults' prying eyes. Not that we were up to anything, but at that age, we did not want to be overheard talking about make-up, boys and other teenage chatter.

Now and then, Penny and I used to catch a bus into Bulawayo. We never had much money to spend, but we would go into town to meet friends or to go to the Centenary Park, which was the main park in the city. It was predominantly made up from beautiful gardens; surrounded by plush, green playing fields. There were several climbing frames, slides and swings across the grounds, for children to play on. There was also an old Caterpillar digging machine, a steam train and a tank, all very popular with younger children. My favourite pastime there though, was the miniature train ride. The train was very popular with adults and children, miniature carriages and a miniature engine to match. We would sit in the park for hours, just talking and messing about in our teenage ways. Penny would have a few cigarettes, as she had begun smoking cigarettes when she was about twelve. I had tried myself, but after coughing and spluttering my way through my first attempt, I gave up and did not try again until I was almost twenty, when I became an irregular smoker on and off for the next six or seven years, before finally quitting for good.

Penny was, at times, very adventurous; this was not always a good thing, as she could be extremely impulsive too. One day she managed to persuade me to cycle into town on my bike so that we could have a wander round Hadden & Sly, a popular store at the time, and something akin to the modern day superstore. You could find most things at Hadden & Sly and as we wanted to venture out for the day and browse the shops, it was an ideal choice. We cycled into town and that in itself was no mean feat, there were several busy roads and crossings that we were unfamiliar with, indeed the city traffic was much heavier than we had expected and we had not cycled in town before, so we were unprepared for the volume of traffic around us. It was quite unsettling. When we arrived at the store we tied our bikes to a lamppost near the front doors and off we went.

Once we had meandered around the multi-storey building, trying on hats, sunglasses and the occasional sandal, we made our way back outside to the street. It was only mid-afternoon, so we decided to pop into a nearby hotel and spend what pocket money we had left, on lunch. We had never been into a restaurant alone before! We made our way to a table and waited for the waiter to approach. We each ordered some toasted cheese sandwiches and cola. We sat on the veranda, near the back of the restaurant, enjoying the feeling of instant adulthood.

We felt as close to grown up we could imagine, and we relished every moment. After we had eaten, Penny and I paid our bill, leaving a small tip because we felt that we would be expected to do so. As I got up to go I saw Penny sneak an ashtray into her bag. Once outside I asked her what she thought she was doing! That was stealing, even though it was small and cheap, but she thought it was hysterically funny and there was no way that I would ever have been able to make her take it back. Therefore, I relented and gave in to her petty theft. After a while, I also began to think it was funny and that she had been really bold in stealing it, although I would never have had the guts to do something like that. I was one of those unfortunates who were unable to get away with telling lies, my face would belie what I was saying.

Another weekend activity that we enjoyed was to ride the 'white roads' and chase rabbits. Penny was by now, more mature than I was, primarily because she had not lived the sheltered life that I had. Being the youngest of fourteen, she had her wits about her and in some ways she very mature for her years. Not long after her fourteenth birthday, Penny acquired a new boyfriend, Sean, he seemed to be a lot like the guy she was with before as he was also a heavy weekend drinker. I have no idea how or where she met him, he just appeared one day. He was also in his early twenties and had a car she seemed to like the much older guys. Sometimes he would take us out for a late night drive up some country lanes, which were known as the 'white roads'. These roads were white due to the high limestone content of the ground. Rabbits were often trapped in the glare of the car's headlights and Penny delighted in getting Sean to try to hit them as we drove along, urging Sean to drive faster and faster. Fortunately, Sean was a decent driver and rarely did so, and managed to avoid hitting any rabbits.

Going into Bulawayo at the weekend was a regular thing, especially as Penny and I were average fifteen years olds, who wished they had a fortune to spend. We would walk around town window-shopping and testing perfume samples in the stores. Then we would come home reeking from the concoction of sprays that we had tried on each other.

It was on one of these trips that I began to be aware that Penny was getting involved in things that she perhaps should not. We had gone into town as usual, and decided to pop into a small, but cheap, café for lunch. While we were there, three friends of Penny's turned up. They had walked past and had seen us sitting at a table near the window. The trio quickly joined us and we all had a coke each. Penny introduced them to me, as some new friends she met recently at another friend's party.

There were two lads and a girl, they were probably about four years or so, older than Penny and myself. After just a few moments, I began to feel uneasy. These so-called friends were complete strangers to me and Penny had never mentioned them before, so I felt a little shy in their presence as they were very friendly with Penny and had clearly been friends with her for some time. I cannot recall their names, but the girl was pleasant and friendly, I enjoyed talking with her.

The two lads were a bit odd though, one of them was constantly reassuring the other that he would be fine. The lad, who needed reassuring, was dressed very sloppily and appeared unwashed. His hair was greasy and his clothes were unkempt and shoddy. He was slumped back in his plastic seat. I could hear his companion telling him, that he would sort it and not to worry, perhaps if he ate something he would feel better. He ordered his friend some food and made sure that Penny and the other girl got a toasted sandwich. I was happy with my coke at the time.

The food did not help much at all, the young man was very pale and he was sweating profusely. He was also complaining of stomach cramps and he had the shakes throughout his body. My first instinct was that he had taken something and I spoke quietly to Penny about it. She said it was nothing and that I should not worry about it, he would be fine when he was 'fixed' later. As the afternoon went on I began to feel more and more uncomfortable and out of my depth. Penny took something from the lad who bought the food and she disappeared into the toilets with the girl. They came back out a few minutes later giggling and acting weird. Penny announced that she was going to go with these people to a party that night and asked if I wanted to come. I knew my parents would not let me go to as they were very wary about where I was when I wasn't at home, thankfully it was a good excuse to get away. Penny made some snide comment about me being a 'goodie two shoes' and suggested that her friends weren't good enough for me.

Very soon, I found myself in a difficult situation, Penny's new friends were asking me to try something that they had with them. They said that it would be fun, that I would enjoy it and that it was not addictive, so I only had to try it once and if I did not like it—then there would have been no harm done. Penny admitted that it was a drug and that she had taken it many times and that 'there is nothing to it'. I did not want to try it, and as the sickly youth grabbed my arm to try and encourage me to take some, I pleaded with Penny that we should leave and go home now. Penny was adamant that she was going to stay. She reminded me that she would be staying for the rest of the day and then would be going to the party at one of the trio's home.

Well, that was it, I did not want to know anything else about her friends, and they were obviously into stuff that I had no desire or interest in. Not wishing to get involved any further in what they were in to, I said my goodbyes and went to catch the bus home.

Now many of you may think that I was a real wimp for disappearing like that. You have to bear in mind that I came from a very sheltered family life, I was forbidden to do many things that other girls my age could do, dating, for example, was out of the question. Only a few weeks earlier, I had spoken to my mother about a boy I knew and how he wanted to take me to the cinema and that he had asked me to be his girlfriend. I liked him a lot and would have been delighted if she had said that it would be okay. However, that was not the case, and I was pretty much told that I could not see him and that I should concentrate on my schooling. Being that I was afraid of repercussions from either of my parents, I went along with that and did indeed finish school before I began dating properly.

This strict family life had some drawbacks, when I was unable to be with friends at parties or events, but it did have its upside too. Drug awareness was a hot topic in school, where we were given regular talks on avoiding drugs and users, by the police, religious groups and our teachers. The signs and symptoms were easy to detect and having had the drugs lesson several times, I knew what I was looking at with that young man. I made a conscious decision not to become involved in the drugs scene, and to this day, I have never tried drugs of any sort. Penny, on the other hand, was already addicted, something I was not fully aware of at the time and did not realise until later on.

A few weeks later Penny came to see me, one evening. It was a lovely warm, dry night and she had come round to ask my parents if I could come to a party with her, at a friend's house. The party was a matter of minutes from our house, because it was in the next street from where I lived. As I did not get to go to parties very often, I was really pleased that my parents said that I could go. While I was getting changed into some party clothes, Penny came to my room with me. She had not come on her own to see me, but had brought a new friend with her. Her name was Kate; I had seen her at school a few times. Kate was a tall, leggy blonde, and when she stood next to me, she made my petite frame seem even smaller. She had a wicked sense of humour and we soon became good friends.

When we arrived at the party and I recognised that it was at the home of a boy I had known in primary school. He had been in my class and we had been on school trips and outings several times. We had even danced together at a couple of work's barbeques that my father had taken my family to, as his father worked at the same place as my father. The lad's name was Michael and he had a younger brother who I knew quite well, he and Penny had dated for a few weeks the previous summer, his name was David.

The party was a big let down, there was a lot of music, nice and loud, just right for a party, but people were just standing about and looking awkward, as though they were all strangers to each other. It was an odd atmosphere and after only a few minutes, Penny, Kate and I decided to leave and go somewhere else.

It was around this time that I had begun to see a different side to Penny; she had always been loud and very outgoing by nature, but now she was beginning to become more and more secretive and often spent time with her new friends, people that I was unfamiliar with. Seeing as the party was a damp squid, Penny decided that we would go into Bulawayo with one of her new friends. She lived nearby and Penny knew she was heading into town, so we went to her house and got a lift into Bulawayo. I really should not have gone; my parents would have killed me if they had known that I was in town at night! I decided to tag along because I did not want to be seen as little miss perfect, yet again! Penny had begun to call me that, whenever I opted out of one of her trips, schemes or would not participate with her in taking any drugs or alcohol. I genuinely had no interest in them at all. I knew my parents would detect even the slightest whiff of alcohol on me and that would result in some serious trouble for me, bearing in mind my mother's temper.

One such scheme of Penny's was to bump into an older gentleman in a store in town, pretend that she knew him, and then she'd take his wallet! Pick-pocketing was not something I wanted any part of, but I did not realise at the time, that this was how she was to fund her drug habit.

Back to the evening of the party, we got a ride into town and when we got there, we went to a nightclub called Je'Taime. I was both excited and petrified at the same time, here I was, fourteen years old and about to try to get into a nightclub for over 21s only. Well, we joined the queue to enter and very soon, it was our turn. Penny smooched up to the guy on the door and he let all of us in, stamping a little ink symbol on our wrists as we entered the doorway. Wow! I was amazed! Once inside, Penny began scanning the crowds of people to find a particular bloke she was looking for. I had no idea who he was and to be honest, I was not interested. It did not take very long for her to spot him sitting in a booth with a young girl. To be honest, she did not look much older than Penny and I, but he was at least twenty-five.

Penny grabbed my wrist and off we went to join the couple in the booth. Penny sat next to the couple, while Kate and I sat on the bench on the other side of the table. It was a lovely place, very bright, full of glitter balls hanging from the ceiling; the booths were brightly coloured in red fabric, and there was a glorious psychedelic dance floor at the far side of the room, the bar was along the back wall and between there and us was the dance floor.

Penny and the man were involved in a heated conversation, from what I could understand, she was upset with him because he was with this other girl. Apparently, penny was his girlfriend at the time and so she accused him of cheating on her. Well, it was all a surprise to me, but it did explain why I had not seen much of her lately, she was preoccupied with another new man! Half an hour or so later, and the young girl across for me slumped over the table, she lay her head on her folded arms. She looked pale and I thought she was very drunk. She had been giggling and grinning, not saying much, but obviously entertained with the drama unfolding around her, as Penny continued to shout and argue with her boyfriend.

Suddenly, the girl ducked her head under the table, and vomited. Yuk! Well, I had thought she was drunk, I guess I was right. It freaked me out! I had never tasted any form of alcohol and for a moment I was almost tempted to try some if offered, but being surrounded by so many people under the influence was a little daunting for me. When she threw up, I just wanted to run off and get out of there. I did not want to see anyone else being sick! Fortunately for me, Penny had had enough drama for the evening and decided it was time to go home. We had not been there very long and when we tried to find the friend who had given us a lift into town, she was nowhere to be seen. Penny and Kate decided that we would have to hitch hike home. Well, that was another new thing that I had learned about Penny, she was now regularly hitch hiking into town and back, a risky thing to do at the best of times, especially in the current climate. This was worse though as this was at night-time and goodness knows who was out there, and although I was not comfortable about doing this, it seemed like we had no choice if we wanted to get home. Therefore, off we went to the main road and began trying to hitch a lift home.

We were very fortunate as almost immediately we were given a lift by a middle aged couple in a Combi Minibus. The best way to describe a Combi is to remind people of the film convoy and the hippies who joined the group in their flower power painted combi. The three of us jumped into the back of the minibus and off we went. We dropped Kate at the end of her street, from where she had a short walk to her home. When we got close to where Penny and I lived we asked to be dropped a few houses away from ours. The couple had been very polite and pleasant to us, and we were very grateful for the lift, but they were asking very prying questions and wanted to know where we lived and why we were out in town at that time of night. In the uneasy and violent climate of the time, it was rare that people as young as we were, would be out after dark. The couple were clearly concerned about our welfare and wanted to ensure that we were going home and not up to anything underhand. When we left their car, we dashed into the drive of the house where they had dropped us, seeing us going into the yard, the couple quickly drove off. We then emerged from the garden and went our own way home.

That was a night to remember, and not one that I wanted to repeat. In my mind, I was far too young to be gadding about all over town, drinking and flirting with men in their twenties, like my friend Penny was now doing. A few days later, when I went to see her, she told me about her latest boyfriend, that he was much older, that she enjoyed drinking with him and that she was also sleeping with him. Ouch! Only a few nights ago she had accused her boyfriend of cheating on her, already she had dumped him and had moved on to this new guy, and at the same time she was sleeping with him already. That was a big deal back then, we were only fourteen and although we would talk about sex and what it would be like, when we lost our virginity, I had no plans of sleeping with anyone till I was ready and with the right person. I had made the conscious decision not to become involved in any serious relationship, until I was old enough, and mature enough, to be aware of the choices that I was making.

Penny asked me to stay with her at her boyfriend's house the following weekend. She seemed disappointed that I did not want to join her, and she told me that he was bringing a friend so that I was not on my own. No way, was I going to be there to meet him, I told her I was not ready for any of that, that I did not want to become involved with anyone and even if I did want to, my father would kill me if he found out! As Penny knew my family, she understood how I felt and knew what I meant about my dad. We were still friends, but I did not see as much of her after that, mostly because she was with her boyfriend at his house, sometimes she was with other friends, but it did not bother me, she was still my friend and I was pleased that she seemed happy for a change.

In the meantime, I had also made new friends and now I began to spend a lot of time with Mary. Penny and Mary knew each other but they did not get along very well, at some point in the past they had fallen out with one another. That did not matter to me, as I was not expecting them to become 'best buddies'. It was not a problem to any of us, it never got in the way of our friendships, I would spend time with them individually. I guess that is one way in how things have changed over time, I know that nowadays, if that had been one of my daughters, they would have had to choose which friend to stay with. We did not have such daft ideas about loyalty back then. Mary was the complete opposite to Penny, she was very athletic, enjoy playing sports, swimming, tennis and was involved in regular training as an athlete.

One Saturday afternoon I went into town with Penny while Mary went to see her grandparents. On this trip Penny did something I was really embarrassed and ashamed of. While we were browsing in a large record shop, Penny sidled up to a man in the aisle across from where I was. He was probably about forty years old, a bit chubby and not taking any notice of her as she moved closer to him.

She put her arm round his shoulder and asked him how he was, as he turned to answer her I could see he was unshaven and surprised by her approach.

'Hello, how are you?' she said, as though she knew him.

'I'm fine,' he replied moving away from her.

She went on to say, 'I had a great time with you the other night.'

'You have got me mistaken for someone else,' he said, 'I don't know who you are.' He turned to walk away.

Following him closely, Penny whispered something to him. I did not hear what she had said, but I understood what she had done by the man's actions. He turned to face Penny and told her she was mistaken in thinking that he would be interested in someone so young. He also told her to make herself scarce or he would turn her in to the police. I am not certain what Penny had said to him in reply, but he pushed her roughly, away from him and she shot over to where I was standing. I would not be surprised to know if I had been standing there with my mouth hanging open, I was mortified by her actions. She was soliciting, like a hooker!

'Let's get out of here' she mumbled, and grabbing my arm she hurried to the door.

When I asked her about what had just happened, she did not hesitate in confirming my thoughts, she had indeed tried to get the man interested in her. I have no idea what she would have done if he had accepted her proposal, but she certainly seemed to be confident in her actions. This had become another way of getting the money that she needed for her growing drug habit. I began to distance myself from Penny at this point, it was obvious to me that she was moving in different circles to me and I had no interest in joining her.

I spent more and more time with Mary after that.

On one of our weekend excursions into town, Mary had me in absolute stitches. During the bus trip into town, I had been laughing with her non-stop over everything from bad jokes, to teasing our brothers and sisters and generally, just being silly young girls.

I remember telling her about my brother Richard, and of his latest 'experiment'. He had a chemistry set full of all sorts of potions and my parents would buy him harmless chemicals to mix and play with. He was always mixing up some concoction or other, and not always with good results. He was like a mad scientist with his chemistry set. The previous day I had come home from school to see an arm sticking out of his bedroom window. As I got closer, I could see a hand gripping a glass beaker, and the beaker was overflowing with the most vivid, orange coloured, froth. The froth was just expanding and expanding, flowing over the top of the container, running down his hand and arm, on to the grass beneath the window. I laughed when I realised that this was another one of his experiments gone wrong. He swore me to secrecy not to tell mother. In the past he had stained his bedroom floor, window sill, bedside table and even his bedding many times, with his potions and mixes. Mary knew about his 'scientific' hobby and we had giggled at the thought of my mother catching him and how he would soft-soap his way out of trouble, as he always did, being mother's pet.

When we got to town we linked arms and we headed to the shops, in high spirits. In fact, we were so carefree and happy, that we began to sing, and we danced as we went, singing Let Your Love Flow, by the Bellamy Brothers, as we went along. We drew some amusing stares and many, many smiles from passers-by. To this day, I still remember how free we felt, and how happy we were, walking down the street, singing, dancing, not a care in the world. I have often wondered what was so special about that day, to make us both feel so good, perhaps it was just the good old African sunshine. I still do not have an answer, but who cares, we were happy and that is what was important!

Mary and I spent a lot of time together, she went to the same school as I did and although we were in different classes, we were studying the same subjects at the same time. It was good to have someone to work with when homework beckons. The girls' school gave a regular two hours a day homework, with two and a half hours' worth at weekends. Mary's parents were as strict as mine, so it was easy for us to get along.

A few weeks later Mary had gone to the country to visit some family who lived on a farm in the middle of nowhere.

She would be gone for the weekend. Ironically this weekend Penny chose to call me and asked me round to hers for cake and chit-chat, like we used to do. I accepted, but with a little trepidation. I was wary of her because of her past actions, but then she was still my friend, so I had agreed to go. During the afternoon Penny's mother said she was going in to town and would we like to go, immediately we said yes and got in the car, excited and keen to get out of the house.

I have no explanation for what Penny did next. I have no idea what possessed her to do what she did, but it happened and again I fell out with her over it.

Penny's mother let us stay in town for a bit longer once she had finished her shopping. She gave us bus fare and sent us off to have a good time window-shopping. We had been heading back to the bus stop to catch the next bus home, when Penny decided to nip into a bric-a-brac store. It was the kind of place that we would go into for belts and big buttons to make our clothes look more modern. There were all kinds of lace and fabric which Penny sometimes bought; her mother would make her pretty little tops with the materials. So, we headed inside to have a meander round before going home.

Then Penny did something really stupid, well I thought it was. She approached a middle aged man and sidled up to him, I can only describe it as sidling, because that is what she did. She leaned in close to this poor old guy, and she breathed down his neck as he was looking at some ties. Then she whispered something to him and it made him blush. When he turned to look at her, I saw the look of shock and surprise on his face. Then he became angry and started to shout at Penny and chase her away from him. I had no idea what she was up to, but I knew it was not good. The commotion attracted the attention of the sales assistant who looked up to see what was going on, Penny looked at me, smiled and then ran out of the store. She was laughing and giggling, as if this was funny, a game of some sort. I was furious with her, once again I felt ashamed to be associated with her.

Sheepishly, I followed. When I caught up with her she was still laughing and fishing in her bag for something. She pulled out a belt that she had stashed in her bag while we were in the store, now she was shoplifting. What was she doing? I asked her what she was playing at and she told me that she had asked the man in the store if he fancied a bit of hanky panky and that she was willing . . . for a price. I asked her why she did it, was it to cause a distraction so that she could sneak the belt out? But the answer she gave me, was a cold, clear No, she meant what she had said to him. Bloody hell! She was still at it! She had just tried to sell herself to some strange bloke in a bric-a-brac store. It was madness, nothing short of complete and utter madness. I did not know whether to laugh or cry. In the end, I decided to ignore it. On the way home that day, she told me that she had done that a few times and had made some good money at it. Now I knew for sure that she was now regularly prostituting herself, and she was only fifteen years old. What was the world coming to? I told her that I thought she was wrong in doing that; I made it clear that I did not want to be her friend unless she stopped it.

It was on that trip home that I really became aware of the extent of her drug use and the ways that she was making money to feed her habit. She also admitted that she had stolen money from her parents. We drifted apart for a few weeks, until one day when she called and invited me round. I said no, but she came round to my house to apologise for her behaviour. She assured me she was clean and had given up that lifestyle.

I was unsure whether to believe her at first, but over the following weeks it seemed that she was telling the truth and so our friendship was renewed.

MONKEY'S WEDDING AND CANARY CREEPERS

Rhodesia was a beautiful country, with beautiful people and even more beautiful fauna and flora. It would be remiss of me not to at least mention some of them, therefore I am going to take some time to tell you of some of the attractive and interesting insects and animals that I came across.

As, there were so many animals and creatures to get used to, I was often found in the garden, watching some new and amazing insect or small creature. We had many, many pets and often they were of the wild variety. Over the years, we had the usual, rabbits, dogs, hamsters and mice. Uncommonly, we had several chameleons, stick insects, bantam hens, a tortoise or two, guinea pigs in an outdoor pen, a Chow Chow dog, and several Pomeranian and Chihuahua dogs.

There was also the occasional lizard or frog that we may have stumbled across and brought home. Several small birds have been cared for, having fallen from their nests, before they could fly. These small patients were lovingly kept in a shoe box and fed by an eye dropper, most of the birds managed to survive the ordeal. I also had two small blue finches; they were the most amazing birds, with their vibrant blue colour and tiny, delicate stature. I often released them in my bedroom as I cleaned their cage; they were very tame and would fly to me. I was devastated when they died, one after the other, from a viral infection.

My ultimate fascination though, was with elephants, no matter what animals I came across, or may have momentarily distracted me; elephants were always the most interesting and amusing creatures. I was fascinated by the fact that they had feelings and emotions like humans, I would watch them for as long as I could when we came across them in the games reserves. I still have the same interest in elephants today. I once saw a film where the elephants were eating the ripe, and fermenting fruit of the marula tree. The elephants were very quickly drunk and under the influence. It was the most hilarious thing I have ever seen and to this day I still smile when I think about it. I suspect that if I looked on 'you tube' that I would find something about the drunken antics of animals eating marulas.

One day, when I had just returned home from school I found my mother in the back garden, staring at a large black creature with a hard shell like exterior, on the ground in front of her. It looked like a snake at first and that is what she was saying it was. She seemed quite anxious to have it moved and sent my brother to the house next door to ask the lady who lived there for advice on how to move it. When the lady came round, she laughed and told us it was not a snake, but a chongololo—very common in Africa. When I took a closer look, I could see that it had hundreds of legs. It turned out to be an enormous black centipede, which is common throughout the area we were in. The locals called it a 'chongololo', I hope that is how you spell it. They are completely harmless and shed their skin, as they grow larger and larger. The discarded skin and scales often resemble snakeskins. This was not your average household centipede though; the thing was at least twelve inches long and looked like a long, fat, black sausage with legs, lots of legs! I was fascinated and sat watching the creature, in awe of how it moved around. Once I knew that it was harmless, I was happy to spend time around it.

There were many, many other new creatures and insects that we had to get used to. There were many poisonous spiders to be aware of, along with the occasional scorpion. One of the worst insects to watch for was ticks, these blood sucking insects which could make you very ill if you came down with tick fever. There were many snakes and scorpions around, so we always watched our step. There were some really fierce ants too! We often referred to the Matabele ant as the 'killer ant'. This was because they are the biggest ants I have ever seen and they have a very painful but non-lethal bite.

I used to sit in the garden and watch chameleons climbing up and down tree branches, my brother Richard used to play with them all the time. It would not be unusual to see him sitting in the lounge, with a chameleon curled up on the top of his head. The strangest thing about Chameleons was that the local black people were afraid of them. When I first heard this I thought it was nonsense and laughed it off, until one day I saw it for myself. A group of African women actually crossed the road instead of passing the chameleon. Amazing! Apparently, back in African mythology, there is the tale of the chameleon that soaked up all the colours from God's paint palette. This allowed the chameleon to change colour according to his background. Meanwhile the nation of black people, who were the last to reach the palette, found that there was only just enough pale colour left for them to dip the palm of their hands and the soles of their feet. So as the story implied, this was why black Africans have pale palms and soles of their feet, and they have an eternal dislike of the chameleon for robbing them of the colours of the rainbow. This is an old tale that children delight in hearing, despite the fact that it is nonsense.

Some of the most colourful creatures in the world can be found in Africa, among those are the bright yellow, masked weaverbirds, and the large blue headed lizards. These were found in reasonably large numbers and were fascinating to watch. The weaverbirds very often fly in beautiful swarms of colour, but the fascinating thing about them is the way they build their nests. The nests are built hanging from the branches of trees, using mud, straw and sticks, very much like any other bird would have done, but with one major difference—the nest was built upside down! The entrance to the nest was at the bottom, not the top. Whereas most birds create a nest with an open top, these birds create a globe shaped nest, with a small entrance hole underneath. This is to deter snakes from stealing their eggs and gives them a much higher survival rate among chicks.

There were also some really gentle moments that I remember, for instance, there was the afternoon that Penny and I spent, watching a spider wrap its prey in a silk web. We had been in the kitchen and were just having a drink of water when one of us spotted an enormous, yellow-bellied spider on the windowsill. It took only seconds for us to realise that it had just captured a wasp and was in the process of wrapping it in silk. Watching the eight legs at work, turning the wasp round and round, was better than any science lesson or nature program. The wasp was not much smaller than the spider was. We learned more in those few minutes than we would have done in any nature lesson. I wish I had a mobile phone at the time, I would have used it to record the event, for all to see, and it was a truly beautiful moment in time. There were many snakes and spiders across Africa; some of them were highly poisonous. We kept our distance with this one, as we had no idea if it was dangerous or not. I suspect it was probably poisonous.

I can remember clearly the first time I saw a stick insect; it was when I was helping a neighbour to do the weeding in her flowerbeds surrounding a small grass square at the front of her garden. I had grasped a handful of dried grass, and was stunned to feel one of the strands move, when I looked closer, I realised that I had an insect in my hand. I squealed and dropped the handful of dry grass onto the ground. My friends all looked up and they soon laughed when they saw what had made me squeal. They showed me that the stick insect was harmless, and I had my first lesson in how African creatures survive, through very clever use of camouflage.

The Praying Mantis, is another fascinating insect that I tried to avoid, the carnivorous insect is unusual to look at as well as mesmerising with its hypnotic movements. The bright green colours would seem to make it a sitting target for birds and other creatures, but it blends in with its background extremely well.

A monkey's wedding was a wonder to see. It happened once a year and this was when all the flying ants would come out from their nests in the ground, for mating I believe. It was usually after a heavy period of rainfall, when the air would smell clean and fresh. With the strong odour of clean soil in my nostrils, I would watch the ants flying across the garden.

The ants themselves were small, but they had huge wings to fly with. The ants quickly lost their wings and landed on the ground, many perished during this process.

Cycling to school often had its drawbacks, especially after the rainy season when we would find lots of frogs on the road, those that had not been killed by passing cars, would suddenly find themselves as a cyclist's target. Often the cyclist was an excited teenager, more interested in talking to her friends than looking at the road and avoiding frogs, or great hairy caterpillars!

One thing I still miss to this day is the caterpillars from Rhodesia. All year round there would be caterpillars of all shapes and sizes, bright colours and juicy ripe for the birds! The number of times I squished one of them under my bike wheels, I cannot tell you, but I would try to avoid them, however there would be so many on the path or road that inevitably, I would hit one. My favourite, was a beautiful red caterpillar, with long black hairs. It was a very large insect, with a rotund body and hundreds of legs. I would imagine that if I described it as the equivalent in size to a ladies forefinger perhaps that would give you an idea of how big they were.

There were also hazards and insects to try to avoid, some of these are the more obvious bees, wasps and ants, especially the Matabele ant that I mentioned earlier, was about half an inch in size and had a bite that could fell an ox! Okay, that might be a slight exaggeration, but that is what it felt like when they bite. There were plenty of grasshoppers around and they were harmless enough, unless you were cycling through a swarm of them, then they become a hazard, that blocks your vision, get caught in your clothing and generally distract your attention so that you end up in a ditch rather than on the road where you should be! The locust on the other hand, was a different creature altogether and swarms of locusts were always reported as they could clear a field of crops in merely a few minutes. They were notorious for eating everything they came across, never satisfied, they would eat, eat, eat, causing damage and destruction across the country.

There was not only danger in the air and on the roads around me; there was danger in the rain ditch at the front of our house. It was a large bullfrog, which did nothing but croak all night long, extremely loudly and kept myself and my brother Richard awake. It would seem that everyone else had been immune to the loud, constant croaking, which was much, much worse than a room full of crickets. Believe me that was bad enough! We tried everything we could to find it in the rain ditch. We would poke long sticks into the pool of muddy water at the bottom of the trench, sometimes Richard would be so annoyed and tired out, that he would throw great boulders into the water, but he never hit the frog, or even dislodged it enough for us to see him and capture it in our small net. In the end, we gave up and the bullfrog remained there for a couple of years, before it finally fell silent. I do not know if it went away, or if it died, but the peace and quiet was blissful.

Apart from the exciting range of animals that were to be found in Africa, there was also a whole new world of trees, flowers and bushes. There were fruits I had never heard of or tasted before. Fortunately for me, I loved fruit and vegetables, so each new taste was savoured as much as the one before it. There was pumpkin, squash, melons, guavas, pomegranates, mangos, and even bananas growing in our back garden. There was a lovely green, luxurious leafed creeper known as canary creeper that I grew from a small cutting. It was a canary creeper; it grew quickly and densely, sprouting small yellow buds. I admired its resilience, even when we had insufficient water supplies due to drought; the creeper grew strong and blossomed.

I must end this chapter on a high note, one that will make you both smile and feel a little sadness for the animal involved. It is back to my old faithful, the elephant, I loved to watch them for as long as possible whenever we went to the game reserve. Elephants are known to be very fond of the fruit from the marula tree. The fruit can be described as being quite similar to the lychee and not too different in flavour. The problem is that once the fruit falls from the tree it begins to ferment, the elephants then eat this fermented fruit.

It does not take much for them to become drunk and begin to stumble and even fall over, much like a drunken man would do. It is extremely funny to watch an elephant trying to get to his feet after several marulas. The front legs wobble in a completely different direction to the back legs. Sometimes, the elephant cannot co-ordinate his hind quarters to the front, and he will find that he is standing at the back and on his knees at the front. At worst, his legs may try to do a 'Bambi' on him and he loses control of his limbs entirely and lands seated on the ground. Let me leave you with that image and get back to the rest of the story.

The people in Rhodesia were very friendly, entertaining and not at all self-conscious. One day, shortly after we had moved there, my father sent me to the local shop to buy him some cigarettes and matches. On the way there I saw two black women walking in front of me, each had a baby on their back, tied in place by a blanket wrapped around their waist and chest areas. This was a common sight and something of a game for Lucy and I as we would play games with our dolls tied onto our backs like the women had done. One of the infants was grizzling and crying, it was clearly unhappy. The mother then amazed me with a sight I will never forget. She was still breast-feeding the child and instead of unstrapping the infant and feeding him properly, she casually tossed one of her breasts over her shoulder, the infant began to suckle straight away and was soon quiet. I can only assume that as an older mother, she must have had several children and breast fed them all, perhaps leaving her with drooping breasts as a result. Wow! What a sight, I will always remember that moment. So keep in mind ladies, that a good bra is very worthwhile as the consequences of not having one doesn't bare thinking about.

Living in Rhodesia was definitely my idea of paradise; it was a place of pure African beauty. I was surrounded by some of the most amazing and breath-taking scenery and had the choice of many historical places to visit. Places like The Victoria Falls, The Khami Ruins, The Matopas and Cecil John Rhodes' spectacular gravesite, among many others. My parents were very good at taking us out each weekend, usually with a very full picnic and some meat to barbeque. Even in times of hardship, we would always have sausages at the very least. In Rhodesia, sausages were called boerewors, or wors, as they were more commonly known. For years afterwards I still called sausages wors, rather than sausage. It was a treat that we all looked forward to.

Our usual picnic haunt was the Matopas, now named the Matobo National Park, it was a beautiful, vast nature reserve near Bulawayo, it was full of wild animals, interesting rivers and had many picnic spots. We had several sites that we liked to go to, and as the area was so big and open, we never became bored going there. We kids had many an adventure there. I remember once we settled down to picnic by the side of a river. We had been there for a little while and I decided to take a walk along the riverbank. I had not gone very far before I came across a warning sign, which read 'Beware of the Crocodiles', I dashed back to my get my father and showed him the notice. As soon as he saw it, he hurried us all into the car and we went off to picnic elsewhere. I remember how quickly we packed everything back into the car. I do not think any of us had ever moved that fast in our lives!

There were so many rock and boulder formations in the Matopas and I never tired of climbing and exploring them. I was always on the lookout for wildlife and would look for traces of animals, footprints, nests or even dung! Often when I came across any dung, there would be a busy dung beetle or two nearby, creating its round ball of manure in order to protect, incubate and nurture their eggs within. I loved to sit and watch the dung beetles as they worked away tirelessly in the warm sun. When I had been on a camping trip with school, we had day's tracking animal footprints and examining the many different faeces that we came across, which is all very interesting if you are into that sort of thing, which I was.

There were certain dangers when out in the bush or veldt, as the countryside was known, I had to be careful where I stepped and even though I would wear sandals or other open toed shoes, I always watched the ground as I went about my explorations. It was not unusual to spot snakes, scorpions and many, many insects, mainly spiders or colourful dragon flies if we were close to water. The flying insects were not too bad, there were so many beautiful butterflies, moths, beetles and not forgetting the multitude of birds there either. My personal favourite bird is the masked weaver, a brilliant yellow bird with a black mask on its face, these birds were known for building their nests upside-down to reduce the risk of snakes stealing their eggs. Their nests were fantastic structures which took a lot of skill to create. Flying hornets were my worst enemy, they were gigantic in proportion to anything I had ever seen in Scotland and when they flew at me with their long legs dangling, I would head for cover. They seemed to enjoy bombarding us as we ate our picnic, but they were soon shooed away by my parents or us.

On one of my forays into the wilderness, behind a large group of rocks, I found myself face-to-face with a mongoose. The small animal was up on its hind legs and staring right at me. I gasped with surprise and before I could blink, it was gone, scuttling over some nearby dirt mounds of an old termite nest. Since then, I have always loved the mongoose and have been mesmerised at the speed that they race around at.

There are many larger animals that live in the Matopas reserve; there are rhinos, baboons, elephants, many types of deer such as kudu, eland and sable, ostriches and of course wild crocodiles. I have been to enclosures to see lions and cheetah, absolutely adorable animals, as long as they are behind bars, very strong, thick bars at that! Leopards, tigers and cheetahs are amazing, with their glorious colour and rich coat of spots and stripes.

The Matopas had a thriving wildlife population, as I have just mentioned and occasionally we would have a run in with one animal or another. A couple of these events come to mind, the most frightening involved an angry, charging rhino.

On the way home from one of our Sunday picnics, we were heading out of the Matopas game reserve when the pick-up truck in front of us stopped suddenly. My father braked quickly, causing Lucy, Richard and I to shoot forward and hit the backs of their seats. The force was certainly enough to cause harm and we were very lucky not to have been hurt. Lucy did hurt her neck slightly as she hit the back of the driver's seat, but she was soon right as rain. I had better luck than my siblings, as I was seated in the middle of the back seat, when I was thrust forward, there was open space in front of me and I was able to put my arms out to stop myself from being hurt.

While we were all getting ourselves sorted out and checking if anyone was hurt, there was a movement ahead of us that caught our eye. We watched as a rhino charged the pick-up truck in front of us. The huge creature came running out of the trees at the side of the road, crashing into the truck as it tried to make its way across the road. The driver soon put his car in reverse and came flying towards us, at great speed. My father then did the same, and sent us flying backwards. Both cars travelled a short distance before being able to turn round and head back in the direction we had just come from. The rhino, did not seem interested in giving chase, thank goodness, so we pulled up at the side of the road and breathed a huge sigh of relief.

We looked at the bodywork of the truck and there was a nasty, great dent in the driver's side where the rhino had made contact. Well, at least we were all safe, that is the most important thing, nobody was hurt.

When I was fourteen, my father took a job working at a coalmine. Unfortunately, the mine was situated close to the Victoria Falls, in a place called Wankie which was a long way from home. This meant that he would have to go away for weeks or even months at a time. We would only see him if he had the time, or the petrol to drive home to see us, usually we would talk to him on the telephone when he telephoned to check on us and see how we were doing. It was during this time that my mother began to ask me if I wanted a day off school, to baby-sit my little brother while she went out with her secret boyfriend. I knew all about it, as she initially said she had to go to doctor appointments and did not want to take my little brother with her. Soon enough she confided in me that she was seeing someone, being that I was fourteen at the time, she knew that I would keep quiet. It was an awful secret to keep, at times I almost felt like I was the guilty one! This is not the kind of secret that any child should have to keep from a parent. I knew they were unhappy, for years my mother would tell me that she would be leaving when we were all old enough to cope without her. Ironically that never happened and to this day she and my father are still together having celebrated their 50th wedding anniversary not long ago.

Sadly, I also knew who he was and this sometimes upset me. Mother was having an affair with one of our former neighbours. Neither his wife nor my father, were aware of what was happening. While my father was working away at the coal mine, then 'Uncle James' as I will call him, would come round each evening to check on us and make sure we were safe and well. This seems to have been something that my father had asked him to do, while he was away. I sometimes wonder if he had any idea what he was in for when he asked that. This was not the first time that my mother had strayed, and it would certainly not be the last.

Anyway, back to Wankie and my father working away. We had the chance to go and stay with my father twice while he was working there. The first time we went, we stayed in a caravan with my father. It was a bit cramped, but we were happy as we had not seen him for about three months. I remember the richness of the soil, it was really red and dry in places, yet there was a lot of beautiful, green plants and trees. We went swimming at a local pool and the temperature of the water was absolutely perfect. I jumped into the pool, holding my nose, as usual as I always seemed to get water up my nose and about choked to death! On this day though, that water was heavenly, the hot, boiling rays of the sun had heated the pool so much that it was as cosy and soothing as being in a bath. I did not want to get out but at some point I did and the following morning I paid for my session in the water, with some severe sunburn on my face and shoulders. This often happened to me, I had many times where my lips were 'sunburnt' as my mother would put it. The heat would dry my lips out, so I would lick them and then they would dry again, and the cycle was set. This resulted in dry, cracked and chapped lips, which developed into ugly, infected blisters that interfered with my ability to eat or drink.

While at Wankie, we went to the local cinema; with a woman my mother had made friends with, and her two children.

We watched Mame, starring Lucille Ball. I laughed my head off; it was the funniest thing I had ever seen. Afterwards my mother was horrified, she kept saying that the film was completely inappropriate for children and that we should not have been allowed in. She would later tell my father, that her friend had no idea about what was suitable viewing for children. For heaven's sake, I thought, it is not that bad a film. There were many references to sex, alcohol and a lot of innuendo in the movie, but I understood what it was all about and so did Lucy and Richard. Well, I tell you, this was just an example of the double standards that she had, one for her and another for us and the rest of the world. It seemed very hypocritical that in her eyes I was old enough to babysit while she was with her boyfriend and old enough to be trusted with her secret, yet not old enough to watch a similar situation in a movie!

While we were on our second stay with father, he took us to see the Victoria Falls. These was such an amazing day, that even now I can hear the roar of the water and feel the mist from the mega waterfall hitting my face, just like a soothing, cool water spray.

We were able to get very close to the edge of the water, having walked through some dense trees and shrubs to reach it. The surrounding flora was green and healthy, and the density of the undergrowth and shrubs, reminded me of movies set in deepest, darkest Africa, where people would have to chop and hack there way through the jungle with machetes, to reach their destination.

As I stood at the cliff edge and gazed over the waterfall and wondered at the depths below, I also remembered that this place was now a place of danger and a known place for terrorist attacks. Only a few weeks earlier, my religious education teacher had informed my classmates and I that two young American students had been killed while visiting the falls.

What had happened was that the young women had taken a break from their studies and ventured up to the falls. They had climbed all the way to the bottom of the falls, using the wooden staircase that lined the cliffside, all the way down to the river's edge below. They made themselves comfortable to read some books, that they had brought with the. It was during this time, as they relaxed, that they were killed by snipers. It was said that the terrorists had been over the border, on the opposite side of the river. After this attack, the staircase to the cliff-floor below was closed and sightseers were no longer able to view the falls from the bottom of the gorge. I had tried to imagine how imposing the view would be from down there, but all the time I had the image of the two women, enjoying this wonderful place, unaware of the danger lurking in the undergrowth.

My thoughts were often interrupted by the roar of the water as it rushed over the falls. The falls are certainly one of the wonders of the world in my book. There is nothing on this earth that can compare to the sound of water thundering over the edge of the falls and the sight of such beauty and yet extremely hostile and dangerous area. Dangerous because of the risk of terrorism as well as the danger of the cliff edges and the water itself. Huge torrents of water churned and whirled around the bottom of the gorge, anyone falling in there would have had little chance of survival, at least not in my book.

When my father was at home he would sometimes take us out to the Khami Ruins for our weekend picnic. Located not too far from Bulawayo, these ruins are a national monument, and worth a visit as a historical sight. We would wander around the ruins and imagine the people who had lived there, many years previously. Lucy, Richard and I had very good imaginations and could come up with a whole host of scenarios to be played out on our family excursions.

Not far from where we lived, there was a local dam, called Hillside Dam. I would go there sometimes with Penny and her parents. We would walk round the dam, looking at the wildlife on the water, as there were often many birds to be seen. There was also a landscaped garden area, with a variety of colourful plants and flowers. I was particularly partial to the beautifully named, strelitzia flower. This elegant and colourful flower was also the emblem of the Girl Guide troop of which I was a member. It was while I was on a trip to the dam with Penny and her family that I fell and injured my back. During the walk round the dam, there is a stretch where the water creeps slowly, round a small inlet and into the park area; there are several stepping stones to use in order to get across to the other side of the water. The water is not deep at this point, but children love running over the stones, back and forth from one side of the water's edge to the other.

During our walk on this day, I followed Penny as she crossed over the stones. They are not really stones at all, as they are man made structures, made from concrete. Each stone is a large concrete block; square in shape and quite high for stepping stones, but then the bank at the water's edge is fairly high. I watched as Penny and her father crossed over, then I followed with her mother just behind me. As I stepped on to the second stone, I lost my footing and fell backwards, landing hard on my bottom as I hit the stone behind me. Then I toppled and fell forward, as I went down I could feel the sharp edge of the concrete block, digging into the small of my back. I knew that this was going to hurt. I had landed on my coccyx bone and the stone had grazed all down my back where it had been digging in as I fell. I tried not to cry or show how painful it was, as I did not want any fussing over me. Penny's mother kept asking me how I was, and did I want to go home. I managed to assure them that I was fine and we continued with our walk and then had our picnic lunch at a picnic area with plenty of seats and tables.

The next morning I was in agony. My back was sore and parts of the grazed area had been bleeding in the night, as there was some blood on the inside of my pyjama top. My back hurt, and continued to hurt for a couple of weeks after that. I knew that I had given myself a really hard knock, but I had no idea if I should have had my back checked after the fall or not. To this day, if I had an accident like that, I may do the same as I did back then. I would probably take two paracetamol and rest up.

When I think of Bulawayo, I often find my mind drifts away to the site of Cecil John Rhodes' grave. His grave is in the Matopas game reserve and we have visited it many, many times. Within the Matopas, there are very large rock formations which are ideal for climbing activities, especially for children to enjoy. There are several that are more than big enough to entice adult climbers to enjoy the challenge of taking them on as well.

The whole family enjoyed climbing up and over these rocks, even mother would climb to the top, carrying my baby brother as she went along. The rocks where Cecil John Rhodes is buried, are very high up and the view from the top is splendid and absolutely amazing. The view from the top of the rock is so clear that you can see miles and miles of open African bush, with its dry, brittle straw-coloured grass, barren patches, thorn trees and anthill mounds. It is a fitting place for the grave of such an important man, as Rhodes was to Rhodesia, hence the name of the country. Many tourists would travel to see the rectangular grave and cast metal nameplate, bearing his personal details.

The climb up to the gravesite can be a bit steep at times, but the unique 'onion peeling' of the rocks, provides natural steps to aid climbing. The makeup of these rocks is exactly as I described it, like an onion, as the rocks consist of layers and they break off at different times and stages, giving the appearance of an onion. These layers are thick enough to be used as giant steps although many are much higher and take considerable effort to climb.

I was fortunate enough to be given the chance to go camping in the Matopas. This was arranged for the end of my final year at primary school and it was a regular trip for all the school leavers and we were taken for a week's camping in the Matopas. When we arrived, the girls were taken to a large dormitory where there were beds for us, while the boys were taken to three large tents set up nearby. We had a whale of a time, cooking our dinner over a campfire every night, learning how to track animals in the daytime. We were able to identify the footprints of several animals, including deer and a large cat, possibly a lion. We examined animal dung as we found it, identifying what animal it came from and also determining the animal's diet.

We also had the time to play pranks on the boys. The best one being the night that they thought there was a lion prowling round their tent. One night the wind was blowing really hard and there was a bit of rain too. One of the boys had to get up after lights out, to go and use the outside toilet. On his way back he thought he saw a pair of eyes watching him. In panic, he fled into his tent and woke the teacher who was sharing with him and a couple of other boys. He explained what he thought he had seen and that he was convinced it was a lion. The teacher decided to go to one of the other tents and ask the teacher in there, if they had seen or heard anything. There had been no signs of animals of any kind. On the way back to the tent, the teacher decided to play a trick on the boys. He slowly crept up to the side of the tent, and scratched on the side of it. The boys inside went very quiet, waiting to see what would happen next, so the teacher did it again. Suddenly the boys dashed from the tent and charged over to the dormitory building where we girls were sleeping. There was a lot of noise so our teacher went to see what the commotion was and found the boys. They were all crouching on the veranda, ducking down behind the low wooden railings that ran along the front of the building. Their teacher was beside himself with laughter, and so were the rest of the boys and teachers from the other tents. However, the boys from the first tent were adamant that there was a big animal nearby, and begged to be allowed to sleep in the dining hall. The teachers eventually gave in and all the boys took their sleeping bags and moved into the dining hall for the rest of the night. To this day I can still remember how scared some of the boys had been, they really thought they were going to be eaten that night. The eyes that the boy saw, while coming back from the toilet, were real. There was an owl known to spend a lot of time nearby and it is thought that this was what he had seen.

One final place that I loved to go was the Eskimo Hut. This was where you could get the best ice cream on the planet. The ice-cream cones themselves were huge and the ice cream servings were just as massive. My favourites were the Pink Panther and the Green Mamba. As their names say, one was pink with a strawberry flavour and the other one was green with a greengage flavour. The soft, creamy, luxurious taste could not be beaten anywhere else. I wish there was an Eskimo Hut where I live now; if there was I would live next door to it if I could.

RATIONING

When I was about fifteen the enormity of the hardships that my family faced hit me. We were not alone in this as many, many families suffered with the sanctions set against the country. While there were many things that were included in the sanctions, the ones that stick in my teenage mind, are the effects of petrol rationing, the poor paper quality we were forced to use. I remember my father's reaction to the very unpleasant cigarette changes and the availability of the cheap, poor quality, replacements. The brands available as replacements were not particularly appetitising. As my dad was a cigarette smoker, he made many complaints about them!

We also had changes to the coffees available in the country. My mother was quite a coffee addict, much like I am today. With these changes to food, drink, branded goods etc., we were no longer able to get a decent brand of coffee but had to suffer the awful taste of the chicory substitutes that was all that was available at the time. To this day, the thought of it makes me cringe, that bitter taste left behind when you drink it, is indelibly printed into my mind.

Petrol rationing was probably the worst thing that I remember. My parents were always keen to take the four of us out at the weekends and as I have already mentioned, we would have trips to the park, picnics in the Matopas or we would visit some of the local ruins or curio shops along the deserted, open roads through the African bush. The bush consisted of large expanses of very dry land. The grasses and plants were not a healthy green colour that we are familiar with, instead they were straw-like and a washed-out colour. These poor plants battled to survive by drawing whatever moisture they could from the parched, barren earth.

The bush in Africa is commonly called the bushveld, but we always used the abbreviated 'veld'. It is pronounced as 'felt' it simply means bush, the open, dry expanse of barren ground littered with cacti, thorn trees and dry brittle grass. There were also many large mounds of dried earth, some as tall I was. Some of them were about five feet or more in height. These were dotted throughout the bush and could be easily seen from the roadside. These were termite mounds and ant hills, home to thousands if not millions of termites and ants. The smaller hills or mounds, being the ant hills.

With petrol rationing, every month my dad would receive petrol coupons to be used when he went to the garage. This system was used to ensure fairness in everyone having access to petrol. He would usually have just about enough to get through the month. He would try to save enough coupons to be able to take us out in the car at least once a month. It was incredibly difficult though, as he had to go to work each week and take mother to Hadden & Sly to do the shopping on Friday nights. Many people would resort to car sharing to eke out the petrol allowances. Public transport was available, but the majority of people that I knew, were families with cars. It was a difficult time for everyone and there was nothing that anyone could do about it. We had no choice but to grin and bear it, making the most of our trips out whenever we had the opportunity.

The quality of the paper used in our schoolbooks and newspapers, etc. became extremely poor. While I was at high school, the rule was that we always wrote with fountain pens, there were no exceptions. Everyone had their pens and a constant supply of bottles of ink in their school cases. When the paper shortage began we found that the poor quality paper sucked the ink out of our pens like blotting paper. After that we were quickly informed that we could use biros.

The books would get worse and worse, sometimes there would be actual wood chips in the pages, causing unsightly lumps and bumps within the books. That was bad for me, as I already had the worst handwriting in the school. With my poor handwriting these lumps did me no favours at all. They only made my writing look even more unattractive than it already was, each time my pen ran over one of the lumps or clots there would be an additional squiggle or scribble. In fact at one point, my teachers had even spoken to me about expulsion if my handwriting did not improve. Well, I can honestly say that it did not and I was not expelled, phew! Of all things, imagine being expelled for poor handwriting? It is an almost impossible thing to imagine happening nowadays, but those were very different times and schooling was strict, with very rigid, and at times harsh, rules and demands.

One of the many things we had to do for school was to cover our jotters with paper. Many of my classmates would cover their books with pretty paper or regular brown paper. With the paper shortages and the fact that my parents could not afford to buy me fancy paper I had to make do as best I could. My books were usually uncovered and tatty, which drew a lot of comments from my teachers who asked me repeatedly to cover my books, and threatening punishments if I didn't. In desperation one day, after yet another telling off at school, I decided to cover the books with the paper bags our shopping came in. So, my books would have green and white, Hadden & Sly paper bag covers. Hadden & Sly would be the equivalent of Tesco or ASDA nowadays and we did not have plastic carrier bags then, everything was packaged in paper bags.

There were also sanctions on the foods we ate. I don't really remember too much about that, apart from missing HP sauce. We lived near to a small local shop, called Joe's Store. This was handy at times and my mother used to send me over there for things like bread, milk and yoghurt. She had a particular fancy for their sugared doughnuts with butter icing. I loved the Kola Beer that I bought with my pocket money. It was a cola drink that was very popular with my friends and me at the time.

One day mother was very excited, as she had bought something from the 'black market'. At first, I was a bit curious about this, as I had no clue that we had a 'black market'. However, on this occasion, she had been able to get her hands on a bottle of genuine, HP brown sauce. We were all delighted with that, as the entire family liked it very much. I had taken to using Worcestershire sauce on my meals as an alternative, even though I like this sauce as well, good old HP could not be beaten.

With restrictions in place regarding curfews and sanctions, things may seem as if they were always bleak, but in fact, it was far from it. Penny and I would bake cakes; lark about with make-up and clothes, we'd jump around the room singing to some song, belting out impossible notes as we were both very poor singers!. We would listen to the radio and comment on the latest music in charts. We even managed to go and see a few films at the cinema in town. It was also useful that my primary school was now running Saturday morning film shows for children and teenagers. We would often go up there and see whatever was showing at the time.

DARE I SAY IT . . .

Have you ever wondered about people who say that they have lived before in another life? Perhaps you or someone you know may have seen, or claimed to have seen, a ghost or something, similarly spooky. Well, I can honestly say that I do not remember having lived before at another time, but I have had strange and unusual things happen to me, particularly during the time that I was living in Rhodesia.

The unexplained events that I had been experiencing actually began when I was about five, but it was not until I was eleven when I told my mother. I will talk about that shortly, but first I must tell you about a time that Richard and I met a very friendly, but mysterious lady, just a few months prior to moving to Rhodesia. We were living on the Isle of Man at the time, but only for a short while.

It was a warm, sunny morning in the summer of the previous year, and Richard and I had just woken up. Richard, Lucy and I, charged down the stairs and dashed into the kitchen for breakfast. We had not been living in the Isle of Man for very long, but we loved it there. We were delighted with the old house we were living in. It had a small garden at the front of the house, but the back garden was huge, with an orchard of apple trees. Yet, best of all was the acres of green pastures and farmlands surrounding the village, just calling out to be explored by three adventurous kids.

That morning, after a good helping of porridge and a fresh apple from the orchard, Richard and I went off to play. I am not sure why Lucy did not come with us, as she usually did, but on this day it was just the two of us. Richard had found a wonderfully intricate maze of hedgerows the previous day, while we had been out playing. We could creep along under the thickly woven branches, spying on unsuspecting villagers going about their daily business. We would play games like, James Bond chasing baddies, or trying to trap pirates. I think the pirate games only came about because we were living on an island. It was the 70s, when James Bond was the spy everyone wanted to be, or be with, depending on whether you were a boy with aspiring spying ambitions, or a young girl with romantic illusions.

We both had wonderfully vivid imaginations, although Richard was often much likely to come up with a new game. We could play for hours at a time, caught up in the web of some dastardly plot that Richard and I had invented. Today we were after smugglers.

"Let's pretend that we have to catch diamond smugglers," he said.

"Why diamonds?" I asked.

Richard explained that he thought pirates inhabited many islands, and they always had gold and diamonds. He had been reading pirate stories as homework from school and I guess this got his imagination going. I went along with this plot as I had also read that smugglers and pirates used to bury their treasure on islands and remote places.

We went out into the fields, darting in and out of the hedgerows, ducking low to the ground, hiding from view, after all we were spies looking for diamond smugglers.

"Where do you think we should hide and watch for them?" asked Richard.

"I don't know," I said, "maybe we should try the other side of those bushes." I pointed across the pasture from where we were hiding.

"What a good idea!" yelled Richard and off he ran.

"Quietly!" I chided him. Richard turned and looked at me and he slowed down as I reminded him we were on a stakeout.

Richard said we would have to catch the thieves red-handed with their stolen jewels.

"We have to stake out their den and see how many there are, then we have to set a trap to snare them!" he said. His imagination was already running wild.

Climbing up the short hill at the top end of the village, we soon came to the fields where the hedgerows were thicker than usual. We squeezed through a gap in the prickly branches. On the other side of the field, we could see a farmer at work. This played right into our hands, as eager young sleuths, we then began to sneak along the edge of the pasture, keeping low so as not to be discovered. Whenever the farmer turned, or called to his farmhand, we would duck, or dive into the long grass at the field's edge. We would lie still and silent for a few moments before resuming our stakeout.

On one occasion I popped my head up and thought I had been spotted by the farmhand,

"Oh no! I think they saw me, quick hide!" With that, we both rolled down an embankment and lay giggling at the bottom of a narrow ditch.

This went on for the best part of the morning, each new person we saw, would become part of the game. We travelled across several fields as we played.

Then we saw a small cottage sitting by itself in a narrow lane. We crept closer to the building, deciding that this was a robbers' hideout. As we approached, a sudden movement caught my eye and we realised that there was a woman in the garden. She was picking flowers and pulling out weeds. She looked friendly and reminded us of our granny, living in Scotland. For a few moments, we watched the grey haired woman as she worked in her garden.

In silence, we lay in the ditch, hidden by long strands of grass at the roadside.

"I bet she's one of them," whispered Richard.

"Oh no, she cannot be a baddie" I replied.

"Why not?" Not all baddies were men, he thought.

"Maybe the bad guys have taken over the cottage and she has been taken prisoner." I offered.

Richard did not agree with this, why would she be picking flowers if she was a prisoner. Hmmmm, I thought, he had a point.

"Okay, maybe she can be the mum of one of the smugglers then?" I suggested. Richard was happy with that, so we went back to our game.

Suddenly, we stopped talking and looked over at the cottage, the woman was not picking flowers anymore. In fact, she was no longer in the garden, she was standing right in front of us! How did she get there without making a sound, I wondered. Two small faces looked up at the old woman and gave her a nervous smile.

"I have just made some tea, would you like to join me for some biscuits?" she asked.

Well, we had missed lunch and despite our curiosity and mild nerves, we felt that it was safe to accept her invitation, so we followed her to the cottage.

As we headed towards the door, Richard and I spotted a grey cat, as it darted out the door and began chasing butterflies around the flowers. We followed the woman as she led us to her kitchen where there was a small plate with biscuits, on the kitchen table.

I looked round the kitchen and admired the yellow and white checked curtains on the windows; I climbed onto one of the chairs at the table and motioned to Richard that he should sit down.

"I like your curtains" I said to the old lady.

"Thank you dear," replied the old lady, in a soft, slightly husky voice.

After pouring lemonade for us children, the woman poured herself a cup of tea, and joined us at the table. We drank some lemonade and ate the biscuits.

I looked round and I could see that everything was neat and clean and tidy, and it all smelled wonderful. I thought the smell was from the flowers on the windowsill.

Soon the glasses were empty and the biscuits were eaten.

"Would you like some more?" the soft voice asked.

"No thank you" we replied, in unison.

Despite the fact that we had eaten the biscuits and finished our drinks, both Richard and I had an odd, eerie sense that all was not as it seemed.

That evening, at dinner, we told our parents of meeting the old woman. My mother noticed how excited we had been, and seemed happy that we had had a good time. That night my mother spoke to my father, mentioning to him that she was unaware that there were any cottages down that side of the lane.

"Perhaps I should take a walk down there tomorrow, while they are at school. Just to be sure that they have not been making a nuisance of themselves" she said. My father agreed with her.

The next morning after we were all at school, my mother went for a walk along the narrow lane. She met an elderly gent as she walked, she had seen him in the shop and Post Office a few times, and so she greeted him with a smile.

"Hello, I did not realise you lived along here." She said

"Oh no, not me" he answered, breathlessly, "I am just out for a wee walk, that's all. I live on the other side of the Church, at the crossroads." He pointed back down the hill, towards the middle of the village.

"Can I ask you something?" she asked.

"You sure can." He replied.

"Well, yesterday my children told me that they had met a lady along here. She lives in a small cottage with yellow curtains and has a grey cat. Would you know who she is?"

"There's no-one down here nowadays, not since Mrs. Foster passed away, and she's been gone some thirty years now. Come to think of it, she had yellow curtains. But that makes no sense, no, there is no one down here that fits your description." he answered.

A strange sensation gripped my mother and she felt compelled to ask the old man if he would direct her to Mrs. Foster's cottage. He was happy to oblige and walked the short distance with her. As they approached, she saw that the building was in bad shape. The building was derelict, most of the windows were broken or missing, there was a hole in the roof and the garden path did not have a single flower in sight!

Mother then felt certain that the old man was mistaken and there was another cottage somewhere. She decided that after dinner that evening, she would ask us to show her where we had been, as curiosity was getting the better of her.

After dinner, she walked with us along the road and up a narrow, familiar lane. In no time at all, we arrived at the old cottage, the same cottage that she had been to earlier in the day.

Straight away, we became puzzled and confused. We looked at each other, a worried look on our faces.

"This can't be right, mum" I whispered, "we were here, it was definitely here. But where is she? And the cat? What happened to the cottage, and the flowers?"

"Yes, it was" shouted Richard, look, there is the gap in the hedge where we climbed through." He was pointing to a small gap in the hedgerow.

"Richard, are you sure this is where you came?" she asked.

"Yes" we cried, at the same time.

"It's the right place, there's where we were hiding too, there in the long grass. She came right up to us, and asked us to join her." A tremble was audible in my voice, as I was confused and a bit scared.

"I know what we saw, and we both saw her, we spoke to her. She was here and we went inside and had lemonade and biscuits with her. She was real; I don't understand what has happened to her and the cottage."

I was shaken, Richard was confused, but we both knew that something strange had happened. With no answers for us, my mother decided we should be going home. She told us about the old man earlier that day and that he had told her about a woman that had lived there, but he had said that was many years ago. He had confirmed that she had yellow curtains and that she had a grey cat, in fact, she had many cats. She loved to garden and would spend hours working with her plants and herbs.

Although this story is real, nobody has been able to explain what happened. The best suggestion was that as children, we were more susceptible to experiencing psychic phenomenon, and that perhaps we connected on some level with this elderly woman.

Another time when I had experienced some thing unusual was when I was out playing with Lucy one day. I was eleven at the time and she would have been nine and we were both beginning to take more of an interest in the world around us. We would often get on our bikes and ride off into unfamiliar areas and go exploring. We would have packed a drink and a sandwich for lunch and away we would go.

The road at the end of our street was a mud bath whenever it rained. Our street was near the bottom end of the road, which then rose slightly as it rose up hill towards our school. Whenever it rained, the dry, red soil and rainwater would churn together as traffic went up and down the hill. It created a horrible, heavy, red mud that would cling to anything it touched. It was a busy road, almost as busy as the main road was, probably because it joined two busy thoroughfares.

One day, there was a lot of fuss on the street; there were council jeeps and vans, steamrollers and a lot of men with shovels and picks. It did not take long to realise that they were going to tar the road. Everyone was happy about it. I think that most of the mother's in particular, would have been delighted with the tarring of the road, as that meant no more thick, wet, red mud trails into their homes from children making their way home from school on rainy days.

It took a lot longer than I expected for the work to be done, as part of the job was to include rain ditches and to put large concrete pipes under the road. Obviously, being a child I had no idea how long a job like that would have taken, but they seemed to be working on it for months.

When the work was finally completed, my sister and I were out playing with a ball and decided to take a walk on the new surface. Part way along we decided to throw the ball to one another as we went up the slow, rising hill towards the top of the road. We were on opposite sides of the road, just throwing and catching the ball, back and forth, as we walked. Suddenly I stopped, I had a strange, eerie feeling that I had done this before. I looked at Lucy and she asked what was wrong. I told her how I felt and she mentioned that she had felt something similar, though not as strong.

This was my first experience of feeling that odd sensation commonly known as 'déjà vu'. I was struck by the reality of the feeling, it really did feel like we had done this before, exactly as we were at that moment in time. However, that was impossible, the road had not existed until this day, and this was the first chance we had to play on the smooth, hard, black surface. I was intrigued by the feeling and wanted to know more about what it was and what caused it. So, I decided to talk to my mother about it.

Later that day I asked my mother if I could talk to her, at first she looked really worried about what I was going to say, so I quickly assured her it was nothing bad. I did not often ask her to sit with me, as I would usually be larking about or have my head in a book.

I told her about playing ball with Lucy, and how strongly the sensation was, that we had done that before. I explained that I knew that was not possible as the road had only just been opened and we had not been playing on it until that afternoon. My mother tried to reassure me that what I had experienced was actually quite common, many people had the same feelings and there was no importance to it. It was just a feeling and it happened at times, that was it, nothing fancy, nothing special, it 'just happened' from time to time.

Well, I wondered about some other stuff that I had been keeping to myself and decided to grab the bull by its horns, as it were, and ask her about some things that had been bothering me.

Firstly, I mentioned that I still missed my baby brother, Adam, who had died when he was only seven months old. I told my mother that even now I could still see his little white coffin, with its single red rose on the lid. My mother became upset very easily whenever we spoke about it, but today she just looked at me with a questioning look in her eye. Then she quietly whispered that I was in fact at my granny's house when Adam was buried and that there was no way that I could have seen his coffin. I told her that I had indeed been there, I saw the doctor coming to the house, in his yellow car with its box like shape, I had no idea what kind of car it was, but I described it perfectly.

I also mentioned that the rose on Adam's coffin was not a real one, but a picture of some sort, again I was at a loss for words, as I didn't know what a transfer was, or had even considered that it could indeed have been a painted picture of a flower. For some reason, in my young mind, I assumed that there were only real flowers at funerals. It turned out that indeed the doctor had come to the house, he did have a yellow car, and the coffin was white and had a painted rose on the lid.

My parents had never spoken to any of us children about the funeral, especially to me. She told me that I had cried for so long after he died, that they would deliberately avoid the subject of Adam altogether. Well, I knew all sorts of things about the funeral, she asked me many questions and I was able to answer them, I mentioned that the doctor had also been carrying the coffin at one point. She was amazed at what I had to say, and yet in my mind, I knew that somehow things were muddled up, as I remembered being left at my granny's house for two weeks, with Richard and Lucy, while my parents dealt with the funeral and the aftermath.

I could even recall that Richard, Lucy and I had to sleep in one big double bed in Granny's spare room. She only had a two bed-roomed downstairs flat, but it was comfortable and we liked being there. I remembered one morning in particular, that we had to go out somewhere and granny rushed into the bedroom where I was getting ready and putting my coat on.

"I have to change my breeks before we go." She said, as she rustled in a drawer and then proceeded to change her knickers.

I loved the sound of her Scottish accent as she'd said 'breeks' and so I asked, "can I call mine breeks too, granny?"

She turned to me with a huge smile on her face, "of course you can" she said, "I always do."

Well, that made my day, I had permission to use a word that I knew my mum disliked very much. Mind you, even though I was only five at the time, I didn't actually use the word as I was too afraid that my mother would smack me for saying it. Nevertheless, I always thought about 'my breeks' in my mind when I was getting dressed or undressed, for quite some time after that.

I soon noticed that the conversation was becoming too much for my mother and so I changed the conversation back to the present. I told her that I had seen some monks in my bedroom at night. She just looked at me in complete disbelief.

"Monks!" she exclaimed in almost disbelief. "when and where did this happen then?"

I told her that I would sometimes wake up in the night, and they would be standing at the foot of my bed. I did tell he that I feared that I was going mad, but she assured me that I was perfectly sane, just having bad dreams or an over-active imagination, that was all. I was just as likely that it was merely the darkness in the bedroom, casting shadows that my sleepy brain had interpreted as monks. She did not really want to talk about it after that, so I went off to play, but not really feeling any better. Moreover, the monks were still coming into my bedroom.

One night, a year or so later, when I was twelve, I woke up with a jolt, I felt as though I was being watched. I could feel eyes on my back. I turned over in bed, looked at the wall across the room, and saw the outline of the two monks at the foot of my bed. Oh no, I thought, here we go again. I pulled the blanket up over my head and hid under the pillow, my eyes tightly closed and breathing heavy, my heart pounded and I could feel blood rushing through my head! I lay as still as I could, not moving a muscle, even trying to breath quietly! I was scared stiff. Suddenly, the mattress at the bottom of my bed began to give way as though a person had just sat down on it. I thought that one of the monks was now sitting on the bottom of my bed. I pulled my knees up sharply to my chest, my arms hugging them close to me. I then felt the mattress give way, much closer to me this time, just to the side of my legs. My legs shot out from under the covers and I dashed out of the bedroom as though I had been fired from a cannon, and I ran into my parent's room. I slipped into bed next to my mother, making some feeble excuse about not feeling very well and having a bad nightmare. Here I was, twelve years old and sleeping with my parents, what a wimp! Worst still, I had left Lucy sleeping in there with two mental monks! Well, I thought they might have been, I had no idea though, as they had never hurt me, spoken to me, in fact tonight was the first time they had done anything, apart from standing at the bottom of my bed. I soon drifted off to sleep, feeling safe in the now very crowded bed of my parents.

It was around the same time as this that I began to pick up 'feelings' when I went to people's homes or new places with my parents. I could sense 'good' or 'bad' vibes; I guess you could call them that. Many of my friends had homes and gardens that would feel warm and welcoming to me, and it did not matter whether they were untidy home with scruffy gardens or an immaculate home with well-manicured lawns.

One day while at Penny's, she suggested that we go to the house next door and have a wander about. The house was on part of Penny's father's property, it had been empty for years and her dad had plans to renovate it into a home for Penny when she was older. She would often spend time over there, but I had yet to have a tour round it. So, I decided that I would go with her and see what she would have to look forward to, in just a few years.

We walked across her back yard and soon we were on a narrow path that took us to the front door. I looked at the house from the front, and it looked surprisingly clean and fairly intact. There were no broken windows or doors and Penny unlocked the door to go in. I also noticed that unlike the majority of homes around us, this house had an upstairs. Most homes in the area were bungalows, of varying sizes, but very few had upstairs rooms.

I went to follow Penny in to the house and found that I could not. Not because I did not want to, but rather because I could not. As much as I tried, I could not put my foot on the porch. Each time I raised a foot to step forward, it would return to where it came from. It was puzzling, frustrating and then scary to realise that my feet would not allow me to enter the property. It was then that I looked into the living room, through the open door behind Penny, it was black, dark and uninviting. That seemed really strange and odd, there were no curtains, the windows were clean and clear, plenty of sunlight should have been flowing through the large windows into the house. I also noticed, that I had a sense about the house, that it was 'evil' somehow. I told Penny what I felt and was sure she would ridicule me for it, but actually, she was surprised and confessed that the house indeed had an unpleasant history.

She went on to tell me that the reason why her dad had bought the two adjoining properties was because the owners of this house had been unable to sell it and he had been able to buy it at a greatly reduced price. We walked back towards her house, as she told me what she knew about the family that had lived there.

Apparently, the family had not been a happy one and there were many arguments and fights, as the husband was a violent man who ruled his home with an iron fist, quite literally. This then led to the wife telling her husband that she was going to leave him. In a fit of anger, he lost his temper and killed her in the upstairs bedroom. Penny went on to say that she thought that perhaps a child had died there too, but she was unsure of that.

Wow! I thought about the house and what those people had to go through, I also thought about my inability to step onto the porch and wondered why I had picked up on the violence that had happened in there. Even now, I sometimes notice 'feelings' in new places that I go to. Nowhere near as strong as it was when I was in my teens, but it is still there.

One night some months afterwards, I woke up in the night. Again, I had that odd sensation of being watched.

"Oh no," I mumbled to myself. I thought the monks had returned, but when I looked round the room, there was nobody there.

Suddenly, I heard something at the window, lying still and listening very carefully, I soon heard the sound of footsteps outside, softly at first, but they were distinct and clear, definitely footsteps. I slowly crept out of bed and crossed the room. Midway, I stopped dead in my tracks, I could hear the footsteps, closer now, just under the window. I quickly went to the side of the window and peered around the edge of the curtain. Although it was early in the morning, there was enough light for me to see across the garden clearly. There was no sign of anyone at the window, or anywhere in the garden. I dismissed what I heard as tiredness and so I went back to bed and soon drifted off to sleep. The next day I had a peek at the flower bed beneath the window and the soil was undisturbed. I was convinced that whatever I had heard, had not been real, as there was no evidence of footprints on the ground. However, I was to hear those footprints many times, and yet there was never any sign of someone near my window, in the flowerbed or on the soft, soil path nearby. This remains completely unexplained, I have no idea who it was, or indeed what it was, that I was hearing so often.

My friend Faith, the African girl I knew who worked as a maid at a home near one of my friends, would tell me stories about her culture and one of the strangest things I heard about, was the beliefs that many Africans held, regarding the Shaman, or witchdoctor if you prefer. These people would practice rituals, ceremonies and provide muti (medicine) for all conditions and ailments. Some Africans had such a strong belief in the word of their witchdoctor, that if they were told that they would die unless they followed a particular ritual or took a certain medicine, they would do as they were told out of fear of dying.

When I first heard these tales from Faith, I did not really believe her, as they sounded too far-fetched. There were tales of snakes, their blood, drinking potions from herbs and plants, some intoxicating substances that were grown naturally and all sorts of other titbits.

Then one day I saw an article in a newspaper, about a businessman from Angola, who had come to visit family in Rhodesia. While he was here, he had taken ill and had been rushed into hospital. The doctors there had diagnosed the man as needing life-saving surgery and the patient had agreed to go ahead with it. While the nurses prepared him for surgery, they found that he had an amulet of some sort, around his neck. When they tried to remove it, the man had become upset and very irritated. It did not take too long before doctors learned that the amulet was to protect him from evil spirits and to ward off the illness that had befallen him. If he removed the amulet, he faced certain death.

The doctor was called on, to ask the patient to remove the amulet. There followed an argument between the doctor, his wife and the patient. Eventually the doctor had removed the amulet and the man was readied for surgery. He was heading on his way to the operating room when he took a turn of the worse and died. Faith believed that it was because the man had removed his amulet, that he had succumbed to his illness, rather than believe that the man was critically ill and would have died without surgery anyway. This tale is not unusual, there were many tales of people who had chosen to ignore the advice of the shaman, and who had gone on to die. These horror stories of what happened if you ignored the advice given, only strengthened the power that witchdoctors and shaman had over their people.

One final paranormal experience, for lack of a better word, would be the time I was laid up in bed with a chest infection. I was quite ill and feeling really miserably and generally sorry for myself, when I looked across my bedroom, towards the door, I saw the outline of two small girls. They were sad, and looking at me with tearful eyes, I guessed they would be about eight and ten years old.

I watched as the girls looked at me, and then look out the doorway, as though someone had called or distracted them, then they both turned and walked out of the room and disappeared. I had seen them clearly, in broad daylight and yet I felt that I knew them in some way.

It was not until many years later that I realised that they were the exact likeness of my two youngest daughters. When they were seven and ten, I had separated from their father and we were soon divorced. It was only after the divorce that I was able to connect the two events, having almost forgotten about the two, sad, little girls that I had seen so long ago.

BETRAYED

It was early one morning in May 1976, my birthday was in two weeks' time. The birds had just begun their usual dawn chorus, so it must have been around 5:30 in the morning. I could see the early morning light sneaking round the edge of the curtains of my bedroom window. I had not been able to go back to sleep, it was going to be a great day today and I was excited at what we had planned. The sound of the birdsong was pleasant and soothing, yet before I knew it, I had drifted back off to sleep. It had been a hectic week at school; I had been cramming in hours of study for mid term exams. I had revised English, maths, science, geography and history (yuk!) in order to get good results over the next few days. My fifteen-year-old brain was ready to explode if it had to study any more!

This was Saturday; there would be no more studying, as it was to be a day off. I was going out with my friends Penny and Kate for a change. We had not seen each other for months as I spent most of my time with my other friend Mary. Penny had arranged it all and we were going to go to a farm not far from where I lived, with a couple of boys that we knew. The farm was owned by one of the boy's (Steve) uncle. We would meet at lunchtime at Andy's house and head out together as a group on our bikes. Penny said we would have fun, lots of fun, and I believed her.

The group would be six of us; there would be Penny, Kate, Andy, Steve, Nick and myself. Let me tell you a little about my friends.

Penny, as you now know, was my best friend, she had been since I had come to Bulawayo and I was looking forward to seeing her today. We had not seen much of each other because of the revision I had been doing and the time I had been spending with my other friend Mary. You may recall that Penny and Mary did not see eye to eye, so I always planned to spend time with each of them separately. At the moment, I was spending more time with Mary, this was because I had become suspicious about some of Penny's friends and her embarrassing behaviour and so I was spending less and less time with her. I did not like being put under pressure to try the drugs that they were taking.

Penny had tried some of these drugs in the past, and as far as I was aware, she had given them up, perhaps smoking a bit of pot now and then. I turned a blind eye to that, as far as I was concerned it was none of my business, and as far as I knew she was not injecting or taking anything more serious!

Kate was a year or two older than Penny and I, but she had a fantastic sense of humour and was great fun to be around. She had not long had her appendix taken out and had spent hours showing everyone her scar and going through the details of her emergency operation.

I had spent many an hour at Kate's house. We used to sunbathe in a very inappropriate place, but it worked for us. Kate's parents both worked long hours and she spent a lot of time alone. She did have older siblings, but like Penny, she was the only child left at home, as her siblings had all moved out. When there was nobody about, we used to climb up on to the garage roof with a couple of towels and sunbathe. It was the most hilarious thing you could ever imagine. The two of us would climb up the side of the doorframe, get a foothold on top of the door and pull ourselves up onto the roof. It was quiet, secluded and perfect for working on a tan. There was just one downside to it though, it was hot, very hot! This was because the roof was constructed from corrugated iron, so after a short while the heat would build up and penetrate through our thin towels, then we would have to hobble, skip and stumble across the scalding, hot metal to clamber back down to cooler ground!

I was looking forward to Kate being there today, as I knew we would have a laugh or two with her around.

Andy and I were good friends, his little brother Martin, used to come to my house to play with my baby brother John; they were both only three, but they played together well and were good friends. Sometimes, Andy would ride to school with Penny and me. I liked Andy even though he was a couple of months younger than I was and because of this, he was in the year below me at school. He was tall, blonde, and blue eyed and always made me smile and feel good when we were together. We were always with groups of our friends and I rarely saw Andy alone, he was very popular. He was always with a crowd of his mates; he was very well liked among his peers.

I had met Steve only a couple of times. He was an English boy, who had not long arrived in Bulawayo and had quickly made friends with people within my circle of friends. The way he looked at me made me feel uneasy, but when I had mentioned this to Penny, she laughed and told me I was daft and needed to loosen up. I admit I was very shy and certainly not ready to entertain the thought of having a boyfriend—heaven forbid! One thing was for sure, this pale faced, fat, podgy English boy, was not top of my list of potential boyfriends.

I did not know Nick very well, but I knew his family as my father had sold some Chihuahuas to his parents. He had gone to the same primary school as me, and although we were in the same year, we had been in different classes and did not talk much. He had always seemed like a nice kid, I was aware that he was extremely shy.

So, on this beautiful, warm and sunny Saturday afternoon, I cycled over to Andy's house. Penny was not there, she had called to say she would be late and would meet us later. I did not feel uncomfortable going ahead without her; I had often met her at places later than arranged as she had a habit of being late. Today, I had assumed that Kate was also going to be late and that Penny was waiting for her before coming on to meet the rest of us. As far as I was aware, Kate had not met all of the lads before.

I did not have long to wait before the other lads turned up and we all headed off to the farm. It was not far away, only a matter of a couple of kilometres and we soon reached our destination. Pulling off the main road on to a dusty, dry farm track, I was surprised at how soon we had managed to get there.

The gateway to the property was old and battered, the gate was very red with rust, and the hinges creaked as the gate swung opened. It sounded like the gate was about to drop off its hinges. We rode on through the gate, closing it securely behind us, and cycled onto the property. I could not see the farmhouse and asked how far away it was. Steve said that the dirt track went a long way on to the house, but we would only be going as far as the pond. That sounded good to me, I liked the idea of a pond, I loved the outdoors and the tomboy in me wanted to explore these new surroundings. I cycled on thinking about what animals I may see and eager to reach the pond.

As we cycled up the track, I could not help but notice that the grass on either side of the track was long and unkempt. It did not seem like this was a working farm and I asked about that. Steve told me that although this was a farm, the property was no longer being used for farming. This unsettled me a little, as I was sure he had been bragging earlier about how he had enjoyed farming when he came to his uncle's place. Anyway, I put my worries quickly to one side, thinking I was just being silly.

Shortly afterwards, Steve motioned to us that we had to make a left turn, through the long grass. I was not keen on that as I was aware of the dangers of snakes, scorpions and other hazards in grass as long as this was. It was waist high in some places. Nevertheless, I was coaxed into going through the grass and after only a few feet, I came to an open clearing that held the most beautiful pond I had seen. There was green grass around the edges, spreading a few feet up a small embankment on our side. The pond itself was clean looking, with some algae, but not completely covered in it. On the far side of the pond, I saw long reeds and water plants that I did not know the names of.

The plants were well established and thickly covered the far side of the bank. The grass around the edge of the pond was green, but not for more than a couple of feet, then very quickly it turned a dry, brittle and brown. There was a small tree nearby, so after putting my bike on the grass, at the edge of the pond, I decided to sit beneath its branches and get some shade from the hot sun. The grass behind the tree was long, reed like, the grass leading up to it was shorter, and less dense, I cleared a space and sat down.

The lads put their bikes down as well and began to mess around with the water, splashing each other and generally larking around as lads do when they get together. I laughed at them, thinking how daft they were and how much fun they were having, I wished my friends would hurry and show up. I kept glancing towards the grass where we had come in, hoping they would be here soon.

I guess we must have been there about twenty minutes or so when the boys came to sit down with me. We started talking about mundane stuff like school what we liked and disliked about our lessons, who our friends were, and what we liked to do in the afternoons, things like that. I do not remember exactly how the conversation turned to sex, but it did and very suddenly, I was unnerved and felt panic and fear welling inside me as I looked at my friends' faces. I asked the guys not to be so daft and talk about something else, reminding them that the other two would be here soon. That was when I realised that this was no ordinary Saturday afternoon and my friends were not going to come.

Steve turned to me and with a sneer he told me that Penny and Kate did not intend to be there and I was daft to have thought otherwise. Well, why wouldn't I? We had been friends for years and often went out in a group; this had seemed no different to any other weekend. As he said, how would they know where to come? He told me that neither of the girls had ever been here before, so they would not be able to find the pond anyway. Well, I did not know that and it made me feel unsafe.

I became frightened and told the boys that I was going to go home and I rose up to leave. I felt someone grab my arm and yank me back down to the ground. I was in trouble and I knew it. I had nowhere to run to, I had no idea if there was anyone else around, and there were three of them against one of me and I was petite. I managed to wriggle away from them and sat on the grass, legs drawn up, my arms hugging my knees close to my chest. Nick did not seem to talk much, Andy was laughing at me and Steve was angry. I sensed that this was his idea and that the others were going along with it, I thought that Nick looked awkward and pleaded with him to let me go home, he just looked at me blankly.

Steve and Andy grabbed hold of me and pulled me close to the water's edge, they lay me down and grabbed at my clothes, fending them off as best as I could I was able to push them back for only a few seconds at a time. Suddenly, they had my dress off and I was lying there, exposed on the ground, wearing just my bra and panties. I had never been alone with a boy before, never mind undressed in front of one and I was petrified. I knew what was on their minds and I could think of no way to stop them.

Steve fumbled as he tried to undo my bra and he became frustrated as his efforts failed, so he grabbed the fabric and pulled hard. I could hear the ripping of the garment as he then went on to yank my panties down, also tearing them as he did. I cried as he did that because now I was not only feeling scared, but also abandoned and frightened out of my mind. The boys gathered around me and looked at my naked body on the ground, I tried to cover myself up with my hands with one arm covering my small, teenage breasts, the other down over my private parts. My hands were pulled away as someone held me down by the shoulders and I tried to roll away. I began to cry again, I had tried hard not to, but I fear had taken over my body and I was unable to move or get away from them.

Steve made comments about me, I know that they were about my shape and size, it did not matter to me that he thought I was small and dainty—I knew I was small and dainty, but he had no right to be doing what he was doing to me! He told Andy to touch me and at first he did not want to and I pleaded with him not to, I did not want to be molested or interfered with, I just wanted them to let me go. Nevertheless, he did and ran his hands over my body feeling my shape and form, squeezing my breasts, feeling the softness of my skin, and sending ugly shivers up and down my spine. He ran his fingers down into my private area and I shivered with fear. How could he do that? I trusted him as a friend; I had never thought that he would harm me in any way. Steve told Nick to do the same, but he would not. He went to sit a short distance from us and turned his face the other way.

Steve grabbed hold of my hand and told the others he would be back soon, he hauled me off into the long grass behind the small tree, just far enough away that the others could not see us. He told me to lie down, I told him that

I would not and that I would report him for what he was doing. He threw me roughly to the ground and told me to do as I was told, or else I would get hurt, he grabbed both my arms and pushed me hard onto the dry, coarse grass. I was already feeling bruised and sore from being pushed around and from being held down previously. I tried to fight him off, but he was much bigger than I was and soon overpowered me.

Once he had me lying down again, he started to take his clothes off, I began to panic and I could taste the fear as it welled up inside me like nothing I had ever felt before. I started to wriggle away from him, but had grabbed my arms and twisted them fiercely, pain shot through me, he was looking at me with the most menacing eyes I had ever seen. I lay still and closed my eyes. I did not want to see what was coming and I cried softly, tears flowing from my eyes. I could hear paper rustling and wondered what is was, very quickly I realised that he had a condom. Well, thank god for one thing, perhaps I would not end up pregnant from this. The next few minutes were very difficult to cope with and I begged him not to do it, not to hurt me, he ignored me completely. At first I would not open my legs and so he pulled and pushed at me grabbing at my legs and hips, forcing me to move them far enough apart for him to be able to get in. I waited for the pain, it was over very quickly and I was thankful for that. He was soon finished and he climbed off me, his short, stocky, fat body repulsed me.

When he was finished, he got up and told me to stay where I was. I just lay there crying, feeling used and abused, scared and afraid of what was happening. What would he do now?

He dressed quickly and ran down to the other lads who were still by the pond. I could hear him laughing. Lying there, I felt sick. I waited a moment or two and then thought I had better get up and fetch my clothes. I had only just got to my knees when Andy appeared. Oh, I thought he had come to help me; I reached up to him and asked for my clothes. He pushed my hands to one side and told me to stay down, Steve had my clothes and I could have them once they had all had a turn with me. Oh my god, no! I had to go through this again. I asked him why he was doing this to me; we were friends, why did he feel the need to do this? He did not answer any of my questions. I pleaded with him not to do it, but he was the same as Steve and forced me down. He said that I was not to worry as he had a condom and I would not get pregnant.

Andy may not have been as rough as Steve, but he violated me nonetheless. He ran his hands over me, exploring my body and putting his fingers into places that I had never dreamed that anyone would! I acted the same as I had done with Steve and tried to keep my legs closed, yet again, it did not work, and he forced my legs apart anyway. The dry ground underneath me, was hard and the short, brittle grass stalks scratched at my body. I could feel his body weigh heavily on mine, at times I thought I could feel the thud of his heartbeat. When he was done, he got up, straightened his clothes and went back to the others. I just lay there, defeated and afraid, at first unable to move. I had one more to go.

I was still lying on the ground when Nick came over. I heard him approach, each footstep loud as the dry grass crackled under his feet. I looked up at him as he neared and told him to get on with it and then leave me alone! He sat beside me and said that he would not hurt me. I looked up at him in disbelief. I was so tired from trying to fight off the other two that I could only roll away from him. He said that he wanted to look at me though, and asked me to roll back. Well, I had just been raped, twice, this person had already seen me naked, so what would a few more glances hurt, after all that was all he wanted then I could go home, or so I thought.

Nick did look at me, he put his fingers inside me, just to see what it felt like, he said. If I had known that he would have done that, I would not have let him look at me, it was just as bad as being raped. He had still penetrated me. He sat still and quiet for a few minutes afterwards, while I lay curled up, like a foetus nearby. He began to speak, telling me that he had not wanted to hurt me, he did not agree with what the others were doing, and that they were sharing a condom. What? I shot upright. Sharing? How do you share a condom? He said they were washing it in the pond. I felt sick again, waves of nausea hitting me again as I thought about it. The pond was not clean, there was algae in it, there were bugs and all sorts of other germs. I thought I was going to throw up, I felt so bad.

Then Nick decided he had been away for long enough for the others to believe he had also had sex with me, so he went back to them. I waited a few minutes, hoping that one of them would bring me my clothes. It seemed like forever before I heard the sound of footsteps coming through the grass. I looked up and there I saw . . . Steve. He did not have my clothes with him, instead he was leering at me and I became afraid again.

It had not occurred to me that they would take turns, or that they would want more than one turn, but now I knew I was at their mercy, I was going nowhere until they decided they had finished with me. Steve was quick and brutal, forcing himself on me with vigour and speed. I tried to not think about what he was doing, this time he was grunting and making weird sounds that he had not made before. It frightened me even more and I could feel myself withdrawing into a shell, trying to isolate myself from what was happening. His podgy, sweating body, felt heavier on me this time. I thought I'd die of suffocation, I could hardly breathe as he lay on top of me, his full weight pinning me to the ground. Surely, when he was finished it would be over, how much longer would it take. Not long as it happened, and then he was gone, stumbling as he went back towards the pond. I lay still in the grass and waited, I had no idea what would happen next.

Soon Andy came back to where I was. By now I was sitting up and beginning to worry what would happen when they were done with me, would they harm me further, was I at risk of being beaten or even killed, because I knew who they were?

Like Steve, Andy had returned to me for a second turn, I was horrified, bile gathered at the back of my throat and begged him not to. He ignored my pleas in the same way that Steve had ignored me earlier and went on doing what he wanted to do. I gave in and decided to make it easier on myself and stop fighting back. I was tired, mentally and physically and could fight no longer. He lay on me, heavily, once again his weight suffocating my small frame; suddenly there was a noise from nearby. It was Steve, he was calling to Andy and telling him to stay still and quiet. Panicked by this I wanted to know what was going on, what was Steve up to now? Then I heard male voices, they were deep and sounded much older than those of my friends. Andy told me to lie still in the grass, as flat as I could, while he had a look to see what was happening. He carefully peered above the grass and looked over the field as far as he could see. There were two black men heading our way! Suddenly the boys were scared, I could see terror in Andy's eyes, he was afraid. He lay low in the grass with me, one hand over my mouth while the other two lads went to talk to the men and divert them from walking too close to where I was lying in the grass with Andy. I knew the reason for their fear, these men could be potential terrorists, they were all over Bulawayo and it was common knowledge that terrorists lived on the outskirts of town in farms and fields like this one. The boys were also afraid for themselves, if they were caught in the act. At the same time, they knew what two rough, black men might do to a young, naked and vulnerable white girl. It seemed to take forever for the men to go.

When it was over, Andy went back to the pond and almost immediately, Nick appeared. Oh my God! Here we go again, I thought, biting back the urge to shout and cry.

Then I realised that he had my clothes with him. Well, he had some of them at least, I got my dress and panties back. I quickly put my clothes on and ran to the pond where I retrieved my sandals. Steve had my bra and did not intend to give it back. I did not care; all I wanted was to go home. As I ran past the boys to where my bike and sandals were, Steve caught my arm and warned me that if I said anything about what had happened then he would be back and he would not be so nice to me. He snarled at me when he spoke and I could see that he meant every word that he said. He also mentioned that he would tell Penny all about it and how much he enjoyed it. Tell Penny? What did she have to do with this? I asked Steve, and he told me that she had mentioned to him that I was a virgin and needed 'loosening up'. Therefore, he had offered to do the job! Andy came along to join in, but Nick had no idea what the others had planned.

I knew that Penny had a boyfriend and I knew that she had been sleeping with him, but I had no idea that she was behind this. I grabbed my bike and ran off crying, through the long grass to the dirt road. As soon as my tires hit the dry, dusty road, I leapt onto the saddle of my bike and started peddling as fast as I could. I just needed to get away as far as I could, as fast as I could, in case Steve came after me.

Before long I reached the rusty old gate, I yanked it open and fled out onto the busy main road, got onto my bike again and cycled off. I left the gate open, not daring to take the time to close it behind me, in case they were nearby.

I was peddling so fast, that I was almost flying as I raced home. Thoughts of what had just happened went rushing through my head, I felt sick and dirty, I was crying, hurting, feeling sore and most of all I felt betrayed. I had been betrayed by my friends, not just one person, but, a group of them! Penny had actually asked Steve to take my virginity, and this was how he had planned to do it, she had known all along that this was going to happen. I was disgusted by it all.

I was so lost in thought and trying to get home as fast as I could that I hardly noticed the old man as he waved to me. He lived near to my home and lived alone, he often stood at the end of his garden, leaning over the gate and talking to passers-by. He was a kindly old soul and was always pleasant to me and waved to me each time he saw me, sometimes I would stop and chat. More and more, I was taking the time to talk to him as he was clearly lonely and in need of company. Today, as I rode past, I waved back at him, trying to hide my tears as I went passed, but I am sure he noticed that I was crying. It was hard to hide, by this time, I was sobbing, tears blinding me as I rode. The hot, afternoon sun dried my salty tears on my face, burning my cheeks.

How was I going to explain the torn underwear and the missing bra to my mum? What would happen to me now? How am I going to tell my parents? These thoughts kept whirling round in my head as I rode home.

As soon as I reached home, I jumped off my bike, letting it crash to the ground. I would usually place it neatly at the side of the carport, but today I just wanted to get into the house and see my mother. I ran up the three steps to our front door and rushed into the lounge. My parents were outside at the back of the house. They were at the side of the pool and it did not take long for me to notice that they were arguing. This had become normal in our house, these two were not getting along very well at the moment, some time afterwards I realised that it could have been mother's last affair that was causing the new upset. However, I needed their help and attention today, so I disregarded their argument and walked out onto the slate patio. Neither of them turned to me as I approached them, when I reached mother's side, she cast me a swift look that implied that she did not want me there and that I should go. So I did. The last thing I wanted was a yelling and screaming match between them and me, so I went into the house.

I wandered around indoors for a while, I could not settle, I was upset, nervous, shaking, on edge and at times tearful. I wandered into the kitchen to see if there were any sweets or biscuits, I just wanted to do something, anything to take my mind off things. I did not find any, so I went to my room. I had only been home for a matter of a few minutes, but it felt like hours to me.

I lay on my bed, my face pressed hard into my pillow, and sobbed. I cried and cried for what seemed like hours; yet again it was probably about fifteen minutes. I felt so hurt, abused, ashamed and most of all I felt dirty. I decided to shower. I went to the bathroom and turned the water on, letting the cold water trickle through my fingers as I tested the water till it reached the temperature that I wanted. As soon as it was ready, I got into the shower and I washed and washed. Creating masses of soapy cleansing foam on my sponge, I scrubbed at my skin until I was red, crying again as I tried to cleanse myself of the event. Thinking about what had happened and the lack of hygiene that the boys had shown made me worse. I could not remove them from my skin, no matter how much I tried to, I could have scrubbed all night and I would still not feel clean.

After my shower, I put on my swimming costume and went back out to the pool. Ignoring my parents I went into the pool and initially I just lay on the surface of the water, floating in a world of my own. The cool water lapping at the side of my face as I lay there, helped me to try and calm down. The beautiful warm sun shining down on me did not help to make me feel better. However, I did feel its warmth on the surface of my skin each time I moved in the water and broke through its comforting barrier. While I lay there I became engrossed in thought, the sound of my parents' voices were distant and muffled due to the water round my head and ears.

Being in the water helped to cleanse 'them' from my body, but it did not take very long before I felt the need for soap to make me clean again. I quickly left the pool, drying my feet roughly on the coarse, arid grass. I went back to the shower and once again drenched myself with warm soapy water. After a moment or two I decided to turn the heat up a notch, as if the extra temperature will do the job of erasing the events of this afternoon. It felt hot and yet soothing, creating an aggressive tingling sensation where I had earlier rubbed so vigorously at my body. Once more, I came out of the shower feeling as though I had managed to remove the layer of scum that I felt I had on the surface of my skin. Ironically, this feeling was over my entire body and not just where I had been touched, no part of me felt clean or pure anymore.

Internally I was beginning to burn and ache where previously I had felt the pain of the lads' vigorous sexual antics. Now I was worrying again that I was infected, or even pregnant! I was terrified and decided to stay in my room on my own. I did not want to draw my parents into my dilemma as they had been arguing all afternoon. I felt even more frustrated with them than ever before because when I needed them they were too busy shouting at each other. I was reluctant to tell them what had happened while they were fighting, as

I did not want to have them turn their anger on me, as has happened so many times in the past. I pulled a book out of my cupboard and opened it up to read. After a while, I left it lying open on the bed, unable to focus on the storyline.

Before bedtime that day, I decided to shower again. I had a compelling urge to deep cleanse once more. I still felt unable to remove the feeling of being unclean and dirty, as though I was contaminated with something unsavoury.

I had all sorts of thoughts and fears going through my mind, most of them were about the afternoons events. Now, I was thinking about some of the things that they had said. Was it true that my friend Penny had manipulated all this to happen? I know that we had fallen out in the past over her behaviour and I knew that she thought I was 'little miss perfect' at times. Little did she know that the way I behaved had a lot more to do with shyness and reservation, rather than a desire to be prim and proper. I often used to wish that I was more daring and outgoing. I think the strict discipline that I was raised with, affected all aspects of my life and I applied this discipline in every day situations.

As I mulled over these thoughts, realisation dawned on me, that indeed my friend may well have orchestrated this to happen. If that was the case, not only was she uncaring, but coldly, heartless and cruel. I determined that the next day I would find her and tackle her about it.

I really wanted to say something to my parents but now I was too afraid—I began to question myself and ask was it my own fault? Should I have realised that I was at risk—even though they were my friends why should I have suspected any other motive than to have fun? We had been out together before, we were 15 year old kids, kids have fun, and we played tennis, cricket, biked together, there were no end to the things we had enjoyed in a group. We cycled about to local parks and sat on the grass chatting, laughing and having innocent fun. This was different, this was not a game, it was not fun and it was certainly not innocent!

That night I cried myself to sleep, thank goodness my sister Lucy was staying with her friend, as she did most weekends. I just wanted to be on my own, I wanted to die, I was mortified at what had happened. Those boys had destroyed me that day, I was never going to be the same again and they had no idea of the impact of their actions.

The following morning, I got up out of bed early, I had not slept well and the only thing I had in my mind was to go and confront Penny. As soon as I was able I went round to her house. I knocked at the door and waited for her to answer it. After I had knocked for the third time, a window opened at the side of the house, a familiar voice called to me. I went over to the window and saw Penny leaning out of it, she was grinning at me and seemed excited about something.

I leaned into towards the window and I asked her why she done that to me. What had I done to deserve that? She giggled as she told me that she knew all about it, Steve had been there the previous evening and told her that I was no longer a virgin. She smiled in an unfriendly and sneering manner. I asked her again, why? I was not prepared for her answer. She told me it was because it was time I caught up with reality, that everything was not rosy in the garden of the real world and that I was not as untouchable as I imagined

I was. I gasped with shock, untouchable! She went on to say that most of the girls in our classes at school were no longer virgins either and I needed to open my eyes and look around me more often. I responded that I had no need to have 'my eyes opened' I knew very well that things were 'not all rosy' in the world, but there was no need to force her choices on to me. I said that she had no right to decided when I should lose my virginity, and particularly with whom! I should have had the choice of when, where and who I would have chosen for such a special moment.

Penny laughed at me, she clearly felt that she had done nothing wrong, and she said that Steve had fancied me for ages and that I should have been happy about that. I felt tears sting my eyes as I shouted at her, the things she had manipulated and engineered were not for her to decide. I should have made those decisions at a time and place when I was ready. Suddenly another face appeared at the window beside Penny, it was Kate, she was grinning as well. She told me that I needed to go home and grow up . . . Oh and welcome to the club . . . . she said. I looked at the two girls and realised that they were not the people I used to know they had become monsters, drinking, smoking and using drugs as they were, had changed them into inconsiderate and unthinking people, I had a word for them, they were b***. I had not realised that the boys were into drugs too, but then I had not seen them since junior school.

I went home and stayed in my room for the rest of the day. I don't remember eating anything at all that weekend, I cried a lot and spent most of my time in the isolation of my room. The worse thing was that the longer I left it before telling my parents, then the harder it became. I had an awful fear that as I gone willingly to the pond, perhaps they would think I knew what I was doing. Afraid of further ridicule I decided to keep it to myself and say nothing.

The following morning I went to school as usual. It was a really awkward and difficult day. I felt as though everyone in the classroom knew that I was no longer a virgin, and that people were staring at me. Obviously, this was all in my imagination, but it felt real at the time. At the end of the day, I was very glad to be on my way home, out of sight from the prying eyes of my peers. Well, I thought they were prying, although I knew very well that they were not and did not know what I had been through. On the way home I passed Penny and Kate, they did not say anything to me, but cast me some dirty looks. I cycled past them and ignored them; I completely blocked them from my mind.

Mary was my salvation during this time. She was there for me, she helped me to get through the way I felt about myself, ridding me of my feelings of disgust and feeling dirty. I was able to cry when I needed to, in time, I began to rebuild my confidence and self esteem. I began to spend weekends with her and her family, thoroughly enjoying myself playing tennis and swimming in her new pool whenever we got the chance.

After a few months, Mary's mother asked me to arrange for her to come and see my parents. I was a bit bothered about this, I knew I was not in any trouble but I panicked a bit, thinking that perhaps Mary had told her mother about what had happened to me. I need not have worried; when she met my parents, it was to arrange a wonderful surprise for me. Mary and her family had planned a holiday in the country with her relatives and I was being invited along. It was planned for during the Christmas break and they wanted to ask my parents personally if I could join them and give them assurances that I would be safe. To my sheer delight my parents said yes, all I would have to do would be to pack a suitcase and join them for two weeks. Magnificent! I could not wait. Things were on the up and I was moving on with life and leaving the trauma behind me.

SAYING GOODBYE

Shortly after the holiday invite from Mary's family my parents told me that we would be returning to the UK, I was really upset. It was late October and the end of our school year was looming in mid December. We had moved many, many times in the past, before coming to Rhodesia and this had been the most stable part of my growing up. I had been in the same town for almost five years and in that time had been to a primary and high school, despite moving house four times I felt settled and happy. It was much better than the moving around and changing schools once or twice a year like we had done when we lived in Scotland. I had already attended several primary schools before we arrived in Bulawayo and I had hoped that we would have remained settled here. I knew that life would be different here, and it had been. I had been happy and I made many friends and I was planning for when I finished school in December.

I had my O level exams in just under a month and now it seemed that the past three years of study were to go to waste as we were going to be leaving in a mere three weeks' time. This was all arranged in such a hurry, that we would sell what we could and leave everything else behind and that included the house. We would be going to live with my Grandparents in Scotland until my parents were able to find us somewhere else to live.

There were times when I would sit in my room and cry about it because I had so much to lose with this move. Although I was only fifteen, I had been out, canvassing several hairdressing salons in the surrounding suburbs looking for the chance of an apprenticeship. Cycling for miles at a time, it had been hard work, but it had paid off.

One day I had been to a salon near my school and was delighted that the salon owner seemed to like me. As I was leaving the salon, my headmistress arrived for an appointment, on seeing me she greeted me and I returned a chirpy hello. She asked me what I was up to and I explained that I was calling into salons looking for an apprenticeship for January. She asked how it was going, and happily, I told her that it had gone well with the owner of this salon. She asked me to wait a moment and after a quick chat with the owner, they both returned and with big grins on their faces and I was offered the apprenticeship I so badly craved. I accepted in an instant, I was elated. I may have cycled back home that afternoon, but inside I was flying. I had a job waiting on me.

Now, my next move was to begin driving lessons, fortunately for me the age of driving in Bulawayo was fifteen, so I asked my father that evening if he would help me with some lessons until I was earning enough to pay for professional lessons. He said he would help me, and not to worry about paying for lessons until he felt that I was going to be getting close to taking the test.

Hooray, I was delighted with myself. All I had to do now was focus on my exams next month, have my Christmas break, which included a two week holiday with Mary and her family and then I was off to work in January. Things were looking bright and I could not wait to leave school and begin my hairdressing career.

Now all of that was in ruins. There would be no exams, no holiday, no job and no driving lessons. It was all gone and there was nothing I could do about it. Furthermore, I would not be able to tell my friends that we were leaving. This was because my parents were afraid of the potential backlash regarding the fact that my father had been called up to do his stint in the army. He had managed to get out of it twice before and now his time had come and he had to do his bit along with all the other fathers. My parents decided that he would not be going and that the only way out was to leave the country, quickly and quietly, hence the secrecy. If caught he could be treated like a deserter.

I felt awful; I was going to leave everything behind, my friends, all our pets, and my future. I could not talk to anyone about how I felt or my concerns about what I was going to do when I got to Scotland. Where would we be living, would I like it, would I cope in a co-ed secondary school? I knew my chances of working and get my driver's licence had gone, I would be too young under Scottish law and would have to go back to school.

I had a terrible time keeping my secret from Mary; she had been a good friend to me during the awful period surrounding the rape and the after effects. She had supported me; she was a kind, considerate and trustworthy friend, yet I could not confide in her this time. Worst of all was the fact that I would not be able to go on holiday with her and her family. I felt such a deep sense of betrayal, because I could not speak to Mary about this. I felt awful and powerless.

Lucy and I would talk about what we thought it would be like, back in the UK. We could remember the cold, the rain and some of the people we went to school with. We both could remember that the secondary schools were co-ed, unlike our current high school, which was all girls and I felt some relief that she shared my fears. We did worry about how we would fit in, having such a big change ahead of us. We also spoke about how we would miss our friends and that even after we leave, we would not be able to write to them either. We agreed that that was going to be the hardest thing for both of us.

We spoke about the things we would miss, the weather, the people, the parks, and our swimming pool was high up on the list. We were not looking forward to the cold.

As my parents sold off the furniture, toys, car and household stuff, I began to discourage my friends from calling on me and would always go to their homes instead. Within days my bike had been sold and I had to walk everywhere, going to friends was easy enough, but it was more than an hour's walk to and from school each day. Lucy and I walked together to school every day and each day was harder than the day before. As the week wore on, we would become increasingly exhausted from lugging our heavy school cases back and forth each day.

A week before we were scheduled to fly to London, I came home from school to find that our beds had been sold and most of the bedding. All that was left were a few bed sheets. This meant that at night we would have to sleep on the floor or take one of the cushions from the settee or chairs in the living room.

Then, two days before it was time to leave, I returned home from school to find that the settee and chairs had now been sold. The last two nights in our house were awful. We had to sleep on our bedroom floors, with just a sheet for warmth. The floor was cold and hard, it was impossible to gain comfort of any kind. Sleep was impossible.

The evening before we were due to leave, an african couple came to the house. They had bought my father's car and had come to collect it. The man asked my father why he was selling and he was told that we were getting a new car. The man seemed relieved at that and then asked if we were leaving the country. My father told him we were not, but the man went on to say that he wanted us to stay; he said that white people had to stay or else the country would fall apart. We need you, is what he told my father. This was a surprise to all of us, and it made me sad to think that in a way, we were letting people down because I felt like we were running away. I was quiet that night, there was very little to say or do, I read an old magazine from cover to cover and back again, because I was so bored.

On the day that we left Bulawayo, I wore my school uniform until it was time to change and go to the airport. That was because my mother had either sold or packed all the clothes I had, other than what she had chosen for me to wear on the plane.

In order to keep Mary away from our house that day, I was told to phone her and tell her I was sick and that I would be round to see her the following morning when I was better. She wanted to come and visit for a little while, but I had to put her off as the house was empty and she would find out what was happening. I told her I was going back to bed and I would see her tomorrow. I wish I had been given the chance to say goodbye to her. I cannot imagine how upset she would have been; when she found out that I was gone. I can imagine how angry her parents would be, at having planned for me to join them on holiday and finding that it was a waste of time. I felt incredible guilt about the whole situation.

When we arrived at London's Heathrow Airport, the weather was cold, foggy and miserable. We had to circle the airport for almost an hour before the fog had cleared enough to let us land. Coming down the airplane steps to the terminal bus was one of the saddest moments in my life. I was thinking that everything I had left behind was to be replaced by this awful British weather.

THE AFTERMATH

I often reflect on how I was raised in Rhodesia, compared to the friends I made when I returned to the UK. My life had been disciplined and in many ways even regimental, regarding the teachings I had received at school and from my parents.

I had loved the weather, the people, and the beautiful places we went to, the many pets we had and to a certain degree, the security we placed on ourselves in order to be safe. It was all gone now and would become much loved memories.

The things I did not like included the fear that I could have lost my father in the bitter fighting that had been taking over our daily lives, more and more. In addition, there was a new and perhaps obvious fear that I had developed, and that was being out alone and feeling very vulnerable if I came across groups of men or teenaged boys. Perhaps that is a normal reaction after what had happened to me, but I did not know that at the time, as I had still not told anyone, I was coping with it on my own.

As I grew older I began to understand what black people had to go through, how they were forced to live. I was very unhappy with how much hatred and bitterness was aimed at them. Daily they had to face hostility, poverty and neglect. During the last few months of being in Rhodesia a curfew had been introduced and any black person out past their curfew time was at risk of attack by have-a-go civilians or thugs. At times it seemed that the police were just as bad. The beatings that they suffered, men and women alike, there was no real distinction there, although more often than not, women were raped or sexually assaulted, rather than beaten. In the townships the violence had escalated tremendously resulting in fighting amongst themselves.

Racism is a dreadful thing and I worked hard any misconceptions I had and made a choice that I would not become racist myself. I felt it was unnatural and unnecessary. My return to the UK reinforced my thoughts on racism and I was happy to see people interacting with each other without restrictions.

My time at school was up and down, I never really liked school, although I did like some of the subjects we were taught, like art for instance. I was always getting good grades for my art projects. I was also fond of some of my lessons that incorporated on different cultures and I really enjoyed modern studies (politics nowadays) were very interesting.

The extremely strict disciplines of school and home life were very different to what I found in Scotland. The belt had been banned from use in classrooms only months before our return to Scotland and the impact of the loss of the teachers' best known method of punishment was very obvious. In the lessons that I attended, there was no discipline, or respect for that matter, for the teacher and other pupils in class. I would sit through lesson after lesson and not learn a thing due to the teachers having to spend so much time trying to reprimand misbehaviour and hostility in the classroom.

There is one lesson that still comes to mind and that was the day that the English teacher walked out the classroom in disgust. Two teenaged boys, fifteen year olds as I and my peers were at the time, had been misbehaving all through the lesson and had decided to jump up and down on the desks and chairs in the class. They did not stick to their own tables, but jumped from table to table as the teacher did her best to persuade them to come down. After realising that they were out of control, the teacher left the class and we were left on our own for the rest of the lesson. This was a typical lesson on any subject, on any day and it seemed like I was a million miles from Rhodesia. There would never have been such unruliness over there; one step out of place and the cane would be waiting for you. I knew that the loss of the main form of discipline had hit teachers hard as they grappled with new ways of controlling unruly youths. At times since then, I have wondered if there have been any effective methods of discipline for the most abusive and ill-mannered pupils.

On reflection I have to admit that although the schooling was hard, especially undertaking bomb drills and evacuation plans for terrorist attacks. The rules and guidelines I was subject to, were necessary and therefore acceptable and I responded well to them, for the most part anyway. I was brought up to understand that it was essential that I went to school to learn, not play about, and that is what I did, as best as I could. Unlike what I found here, where it almost felt as though children went to school to get out of the way of mum and dad, the importance of having good education seemed to have slipped their minds, but more than likely as I suspected—that it was never there.

Although here in my tale, I have mentioned only a couple of schools, I did attend fifteen schools and colleges in total, not counting the two Universities that I studied with as a mature student. This constant change and moving from place to place and from school to school, had an effect on my personality. I was always quiet and withdrawn, only making one or two friends and not really mixing with many of my peers. I put this down to always being the 'new girl'. When I was younger I found it increasingly difficult to leave my friends behind when the family moved, and so I distanced myself and did not form close friendships. I stayed like that for many years. I was a bit of a loner and suspect that I still am, as even in adulthood, I still only ever had one or perhaps two friends at a time.

Another very good reason, for only having one or two friends at a time, is to reduce the risk of harm, after all, I had trusted Penny and yet she had set me up with those lads as a means of converting me to her way of teenage life. She was a sexually active teen but that did not mean that I wanted to be. The choice on something like that has to rest with the individual; it is not something that a friend can decide for you.

Later I was to find out that she had offered sex to one of our neighbours, as payment for giving her a lift home from the town centre. My father had been so relieved to know that at the time, I was no longer friends with her, and I am sure if he knew what had happened to me, things would have very quickly become extremely nasty. Penny's elderly parents would have been no match for my father's anger.

This betrayal stayed with me for years and although I did eventually go on to have many friends, I found that I was unable to share close thoughts or fears with anyone. My trust in others was completely gone, it had been entirely demolished by the antics of a handful of teenagers, who thought only of themselves and not the impact of their actions on me. Even now, years later, I have not forgiven any of them for what happened, but especially Penny.

In retrospect though there was something positive out of my schooling, I had identified that I was definitely not racist. I worked hard at ignoring the way that we were being bullied, and at times, emotionally blackmailed, into only mixing with 'our own kind'. Over the years, I am proud to say that I have many friends who would turn my poor teachers' hair grey, those who had different skin colours, sexual preferences, or were foreigners were all taboo. We even had intolerances in religion, with the old protestant v catholic nonsense. We are all different and we should be proud of that, as it would be a very dull world if we were not.

Looking at how little money my parents had when they were raising us, I soon realised that even penny counts and when I had my own family, I worked hard at saving money and making it stretch. There were times when I wondered if I would ever be well off, or even have just enough to get buy and have a few pennies that I could try and save for a rainy day. Well, hard work and many years on, I found that I was indeed, comfortably off. I certainly have an appreciation of the 'have and have not's', that is something I will always be aware of.

One of the most interesting things that I can say I was able to do was learn how to hold and use a rifle. The thought of pointing a gun at someone and then pull the trigger was horrifying, but it was an essential lesson for me, to help keep our family safe in my father's absence.

Twenty years on, I was living on a farm in South Africa and my husband at the time, taught me how to shoot a 9mm and a .22 rifle. We had a shotgun under the bed and a pistol in the car. My eldest daughter was just eight and she was a very good shot with the .22 rifle. I was unhappy at the thought that a child, so young, should have to learn to defend herself in that way. It was not much later that we moved to England, where I felt safer and less fearful for my children's futures. Although logic dictates that I should have felt safer with guns around me, I did not. I was fearful at the thought that they could also be used against us, particularly if they fell into the wrong hands or were taken from us in an attack or burglary.

Following the attack, I had become a painfully shy, quiet, insecure and timid young woman. I was unable to argue with anyone, as I would burst into floods of tears at the sounds of raised voices. Most of the time, I felt as though I was invisible.

I suspect that this event had been the catalyst for my ill-fated first marriage. I was overwhelmed that someone seemed to care so much for me, unfortunately it turned out that what I had mistaken for love and care was actually his aggressive and controlling nature. A few months after we married he began to hit me; this was something that I was to endure for another six years before finally, finding the strength to leave him.

First, I had a nervous breakdown and became agoraphobic and my life slowly, fell apart. Agoraphobia is the inability to go out into open spaces, this is not as uncommon as I had thought when I had it, but as time went on I realised that I was not going mad, just that I was ill, very ill. Alongside that illness, I had great difficulty being in a room of more than three people, especially if they were men. This put a dreadful strain on my already shaky marriage.

I can remember one occasion where I felt completely out of my depth. It had been when I was I was working as a checkout operator at a local supermarket. I was on the rota for early lunch one day. I secured my till and went upstairs to the staff room. It was a fairly small room between the canteen and the ladies toilets. There were several tables scattered around and on three of the walls were the staff lockers. On this day I had to go across the staffroom to reach my locker at the far end. As soon as I entered the room I realised that there were half a dozen warehouse men sitting at a corner table. I stopped dead in my tracks, panic welled up inside me. I developed palpitations and my palms instantly became sweaty. I found it hard to breathe as my throat seemed to close up on me. I made a mad dash to the ladies toilets and once inside the door I felt immediate relief. At the same time I felt utterly foolish. What was wrong with me? This happened several times and although it began to happen less often I found that the main trigger was teenaged boys and I think that was for obvious reasons. This eased considerably when I underwent the therapy sessions and was soon a thing of the past.

While I was ill with the agoraphobia I was given tablets from my GP, but after a couple of years and the condition worsening, the only help from my doctor was to increase the dosage of the Librium that I was taking. Of all the things that happened to me and that I may have had to go through, the worst event was obviously when I was raped. All these years later and I was still unable to cope with what had happened. I finally told my doctor about it and she organised for me to undergo therapy for it. I also had hypnotherapy in order to deal with the panic attacks and anxiety which had plagued me for several years.

My first session with my hypnotherapist was the hardest, I had to walk to her offices as I was unable to go on a bus, due to my fear of crowds and groups of people. I cried my way through the session but by the end of it, I could see the possibility of getting better. It took eighteen months for me to get to something near normal, I still had difficulties in crowds but at least I was able to cope with groups of people, albeit in small groups of no more than six or seven people.

Over the months of my treatment it became clear that I was still trying to cope with the aftermath of being raped at such a young age, by people that I should have been able to trust. The aggression and violence I was accepting from my husband was in part due to the fact that I had no feelings of self worth or confidence, that it was almost normal for me. I had grown up in a household, where physical punishment was the norm and so it was easy for me to accept my husband's abuse. Throughout my therapy, I became more and more aware of the person I should have been, rather than who I had become and I set a goal that I wanted to achieve. The goal I had, was simple, to become me, the way I chose to see myself in the future.

Fortunately for me, it worked, and I soon found the strength to leave my husband and take my daughter with me. From the day I left him, I did not take another Librium again. I was well again and more than capable of being a good, loving, single mum.

I steadily found the strength to stand up for myself; I had always followed the instructions of my parents, my teachers and then my husband. Through the treatment I was having, it very quickly became obvious that I had lost my individuality, my own identity and obeyed the commands of others easily. At this time it was my husband. I had to learn to say 'no', this was not easy as I always said yes, no matter how busy, tired, or unwilling I may have been. The first time I said no to something I had been asked to do, was a liberating experience and so, as time went on, my confidence came flooding back.

Finally, I need to say that all these things shaped me as the person I am today. In many ways I developed the courage and determination needed to survive living through so many negative experiences. Living through such difficult times should have helped me to grow into a strong, confident and perhaps more self-assured young woman.

Time is a great healer, so they say, and they are right. Now I find that a confident, determined and honest person has emerged from the chaos that had been my life. I have become a bit of a stickler for the rules, someone that hates being lied to and better still, I am completely and deeply committed to my current husband. He is someone who would never dream of abusing or hurting anyone, whether man, woman or child. We make a good team and are fortunate to have found each other. I am not going to go all soppy, I just want to show that no matter how hard things get, there are always ways to change things and improve your circumstances.

There are some things that remain difficult to cope with, even today. I find that I am unable to watch certain scenes in films or programmes, where there is violence to women; occasionally love scenes will upset me too. There is no real trigger for this, it just happens—when it does I either change the channel, or leave the room for a moment or two, whichever is easiest at the time.

This is where my tales end and you will find me happy and well balanced despite the upheavals I have had. There is a saying that life has a way of giving you challenges to overcome, but never more than you can handle. Well, I guess that may be true, it just takes time and perseverance, but we all get there in the end.